SCOTLAND

Celebrations and Soul Food

JEAN MUIR

Matador
9 Priory Business Park
Kibworth Beauchamp
Leicestershire LE8 0RX, UK
Tel: (+44) 116 279 2299
Fax: (+44) 116 279 2277
Email: books@troubador.co.uk
Web: www.troubador.co.uk/matador

ISBN 978 1784620 684

British Library Cataloguing in Publication Data.
A catalogue record for this book is available from the British Library.

Typeset in Goudy Old Style and Memoir by Troubaor Publishing Ltd
Design by Troubador Publishing Ltd

Printed and bound by Gutenberg Press

Matador is an imprint of Troubador Publishing Ltd

Thanks

Many, Many Thanks
To all my family
and to friends old & new.

Special thanks to everyone who:

- Listened to my crazy ideas, watched my kids, tasted my food and told me to keep going anyway, especially Leanne Love, Kirsty Foyle, Hazel Forker, Alex White and of course Mandy Wilkie.

- Didn't hesitate to call, text or email family & friends to help me out – even if they hadn't spoken for years!

- Took me under their wing at an event and shared their knowledge stories & traditions, particularly Johan Adamson, Erica & Bryan Pearson, Bill & Elspeth Luke and of course Susan Robinson, Kenny & Shirley Pirie.

- I leaned on for professional help, in particular Cara Shanley & Andi Collington. But Caroline Copeland, it was you who carried this project from a dream to reality, many thanks my wonderful friend.

- Made the process of publishing and production so wonderful, in particular the brilliant and patient Terry Compton and all the fabulous staff at Matador.

To my husband Colin Muir, my best friend and biggest supporter and to my kids Niamh & Ronan whose patience I pushed far beyond the limit. To 'The Powers That Be' for making this possible in the first place, I am forever indebted.

I feel very blessed to have so many wonderful, fun and interesting people in my life.

Thank you,

Jean

Contents

January – March

April – June

July – September

October – December

Contents

Introduction

I live in a beautiful land filled with history, culture and intrigue. My journey of trying to learn and understand about the people and cultures in my adopted homeland has been such a rich and joyous ride. I can't wait to share some of them with you, but let's back up a bit first.

Sunset at Loch Tay, Awaiting the Closing of Salmon Season

A Bit of Background

My name is Jean, but to most people I am now known as "Jean, American Jean", as I hail from the United States but now live in Scotland. I first visited Scotland in 1998 to study architectural conservation treatments (high times I know). Whilst the course was indeed a legitimate chapter in a very long Master's degree, it was also a socially acceptable break from a crummy chapter in my life. Scotland was not where I was trying to get to or indeed anyplace I had been particularly curious about despite some family heritage, but it was only a matter of days before I had totally and completely fallen in love with the place. The landscape, the light, the history, the people, the humour, the kilts ... the works!

When you study the history of buildings, by default you study the history of the people and cultures that built them. (This was in a time before I realised I was far more interested in people than buildings.) And let me tell you something, the study of the history and culture of Scotland is like going down the proverbial rabbit hole. It is just so rich, so weird, so varied and so incredibly long, it continues to dazzle me even after years of research. So how does this lead to you having this book in your hand?

A Bit About Food

Of my many passions, food and history and even food history have been right up there for most of my life. When I was about twelve, I had a seminal experience that brought these things together for the first time – I was invited to a Passover Seder. For those of you not in the know, the Seder is a Jewish ritual meal in which every element on the table represents a part of Jewish History: and the eating of the meal reaffirms the teachings underpinning the celebration and also teaches the children (and any guests) that history as well. I confess I don't recall the culinary aspects of the meal but I thought the whole event was absolutely the coolest thing ever. It opened up another world to me and led me to want to find out more: not only about this culture, but the role food plays in all of our lives. The official name for this line of study is *Foodways*, which is understood as the social science of food, culture, history and tradition, but my take on it is decidedly more free-wheeling!

I have been very blessed in my life to have had a wide range of culinary experiences and even a decent amount of travel (for an American anyway). My eating adventures have taken me from fine dining in Napa Valley and New York City, to Jambalaya at Jazzfest in New Orleans, or enjoying an authentic Clam Bake outside Boston. Wherever I went I would try to eat what the locals ate and always treated myself to at least one cookbook as a souvenir from anywhere I visited. Any place, any country, any weekend at a friend's house, a food experience was usually the highlight.

After a solid decade of working with leaky roofs, mortar samples and surveying cracks on historic buildings, I finally packed it in and focused on food for real. I started as a personal chef whilst still in the States and later continued in cafes, catering, and as a development chef in Scotland. Motherhood persuaded me that standing for eight to twelve hours every day was not such a good idea, so now I have a food and lifestyle blog called **Alba Living** and an artisan food business entitled **Alba Flavour** that I run from home. **'Alba'** is not only the Gaelic name for Scotland, but also it refers more specifically to the historical name for the region where I currently live: the southern Kingdom of the Picts – fun facts.

Food in Scotland

Even though I had briefly met my husband on that first trip to Scotland, it was several years and a few star-crossed exchanges before love blossomed and I found myself relocating here full time. I arrived on the first of June 2003, and my lovely new mother-in-law (we had just eloped) had us over for dinner and served strawberries and cream for dessert. *Holy...freaking... frijoles* – I had never had anything resembling a strawberry in all my life that was even *remotely* close to the taste sensation of that dessert. And it didn't stop there, really simple things like butter, actually had flavour! The greens, the fruit, the fish, the meats, were all just so fresh and intense that I found myself positively over-whelmed. I confess I had the same notion of Scottish food that most might of haggis and porridge, but the produce that I encountered just didn't compute with that image at all.

An explosive taste sensation – Scottish Strawberries.

Since then, I have been conducting ongoing comparison tests with farmers markets in Montreal, the Hamptons, the south of France, and I maintain that the core produce and food resources of Scotland are the best I have ever had. However, for a whole variety of very complicated reasons most Scots are, a) unaware of how fantastic their foodstuffs are and b) only eat a limited range of those resources. Well, we shall see about *that*!

The Celebrations

There is a great line from the movie Beetlejuice where the young girl Lydia muses on why she can see the ghosts to whom she is talking. She explains, "Well, I've read through that *Handbook for the Recently Deceased*, it says that live people ignore the strange and unusual ...I myself am strange and unusual." Personally, I prefer the term 'charmingly eccentric' but I do seem to be drawn to somewhat different interests than most. And in terms of the strange and unusual, the unique celebrations of Scotland get the blue ribbon for sure. Beginning with that *first* visit in 1998 when I was told about the **Burning of the Clavie** in Burghead (p. 19), to the time when my future husband sent me links about the **Burry Man of South Queensferry** (p.103) during our courtship, I could not get over just how fabulously bizarre and wonderful some Scottish traditions were.

Up Helly Aa 2013

Introduction

So, as you do, I set my cap to travel the country to attend as many of these signature Scottish celebrations as I could. I wanted to research and photograph them, and also try to soak up as much of the spirit of the events so that I could better understand and convey the experience to others. OK, maybe it was a bit of an excuse to go and see **Up Helly Aa** (p.35) in Shetland, but sometimes you just have to go for it! And while I am sure it is lovely to go to Thailand for the **Full Moon Party** or to Rio de Janeiro for **Carnival** (both of which I have every intention of doing one day), I assure you that Scotland is chock full of spectacular and unique events.

When I started this project my intention was to learn what foods were served or associated with each event, so that I could then present authentic recipes so you too could have your own Scottish inspired events, wherever you may be in the world. However, I soon discovered that there were few, or no specific foods that absolutely had to be served or eaten at any given event. Not daunted in the least, and since in my humble opinion there is no point in having a festival without a feast, I have created my own recipes inspired by the location, season or nature of each event. The dishes in the

x

book are absolutely not traditional and a Scottish granny will likely not recognise them, but there is some method to my madness.

To draw upon this departure from traditional Scottish food, I am borrowing the term *Soul Food*, from its origins in the American South. The term was first employed to signify the food that slaves created using whatever was on-hand or could be trapped or caught, and using individual creativity, would pour their heart and soul into their food to impart flavour and nutrition. *Soul food* can sometimes be humble food, but with the addition of love, it can strike a chord deep inside you like few other things can.

The ingredients that I use in this book are as often as possible native to, or cultivated in Scotland. I combine these Scottish ingredients with the history and culture of the land that produces them *with* my own inspirations and techniques, to bring to you fresh, inspiring and most of all, delicious dishes that I hope will reflect the spirit of these uniquely Scottish events. In other words as a New Scot myself, may I present a new *Scottish Soul Food* to go with these extraordinary and often ancient cultural events!

I hope you enjoy,

Jean *(aka American Jean)*

The author at Wickerman festival

EVENT GUIDE

UK WIDE
New Year (Hogmanay)
Shrove Tuesday/ Pancake Day
Easter
Halloween
Bonfire Night
Christmas

SCOTLAND WIDE
Burn's Night
Highland Games
St. Andrew's Day

REGIONAL OR MOVEABLE EVENTS
Salmon Season
Gala Days
Border Ridings
National Mod

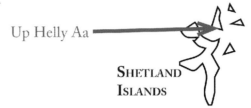

Up Helly Aa

SHETLAND ISLANDS

Kirkwall Ba Game

ORKNEY ISLANDS

Burning of the Clavie

OUTER HEBRIDES

INVERNESS

ABERDEEN

INNER HEBRIDES

DUNDEE
PERTH

Treaty of Arbroath

T In The Park

The Burry Man

EDINBURGH

Beltane

GLASGOW

Edinburgh Tattoo
Fringe Festival

Royal Highland Show

Jedburgh Ba Game

The Wickerman Festival

KEY
January - March
April - June
July - September
October - December

The Burning of the Clavie at Burghhead

January
—
March

Fireworks over Calton Hill
Photo by Robbie Shade

Biggar Bonfire –
Photo by A McLachlan Photography

Hogmanay!

27th December – 2nd January

Welcome to Scotland, a land of people that really like a good party! On the stroke of midnight on New Year, or Hogmanay as it is known here, and with the bells ringing, the fireworks blasting and countries across the globe singing out the words of our national bard's Auld Lang Syne, we begin our journey around the calendar and around the country to see just how we party in Scotland.

It is a weird, wild and wonderful journey I assure you!

But before we go, we have Hogmanay to celebrate! As the bells ring out to welcome the New Year you may be enjoying a fireworks display, or the shockingly large bonfire in Biggar,

Or even the breath-taking display of a swinging fireball in Stonehaven,

But wherever you are it is a time to make much noise to scare away any bad luck and joyously welcome the good luck for a new year.

During the Protestant Reformation in the 16th Century, Christmas was supressed and even outlawed in Scotland. Not to be dissuaded, the canny Scots just shifted many of the celebrations, parties, visiting and feasting to the New Year, a safe distance away from anything that could be considered Papist. Thus Hogmanay became the biggest event of the year, far eclipsing Christmas, which was not returned as a public holiday in Scotland until 1958.

January — March

Hogmany
27th December
- 2nd January

5

The term Hogmanay derives from the name for the gifts that were exchanged between family and friends. Whether the origin of the word derives from the Normans or Gaelic is up for debate, but the overall celebration is now known collectively for these exchanged gifts.

After welcoming the New Year, it is then time to welcome First Footers to your home. It is thought that the first person to enter your door after the New Year will bring either good luck or bad, so ensuring a proper First Footer is paramount. They should be male, preferably tall, dark hair and handsome (whose eyebrows should not meet), of good character and they should always be bearing a gift – never empty handed. The most common gifts are bottles of whisky for cheer, some coal for warmth, or a dense fruit cake known as black bun for prosperity. It is not uncommon for one soul in a roaming group of First Footers to be shoved to the front at each stop. The visiting and merriment can go on all night and often throughout the next day, and into the next night. This is the biggest blow-out of the year and nobody wants to miss a moment!

As dawn arrives, the truly adventurous can take a jump into the freezing waters that surround Scotland as part of the Looney Dook. It is often to raise funds for charity nowadays, but standing on the side-lines cheering is just enough for me thanks.

So, our year of excitement has begun!

Let me take you on a journey through some of the absolute wildest things I have ever seen in my life...

January – March

Hogmany
27th December
- 2nd January

Hogmanay Beef Stew with Red Currant Jam & Wholemeal Bread Rolls

Serves 8

As your First Footers will be the harbingers of your good luck for the entire year, you want to do your part to welcome them properly. Most people tend to serve a Steak Pie on New Year but this recipe will elevate that tradition to the next level and ensure that everyone is deliciously sustained for the duration of the festivities. Serve in mugs with bread rolls or bannocks on the side for ease of serving the roving and merry crowd!

For the Beef Stew

1 large onion, diced
2 large carrots, diced
300 grams/ ½ pound of mushrooms, sliced
2 cloves garlic, minced
2 cubes/ or 2 tablespoons beef boullion
500 ml water
15 grams/ 1 tablespoon tomato puree
3 bay leaves
15 ml/ 1 tablespoon Herbs de Provence
75 cl/ 1 bottle full bodied red wine
800 grams or 1 ½ pounds steak, cubed
250 grams flour – for coating beef
10 ml/ 2 teaspoons cracked black pepper – for flour seasoning
30 grams/ 2 tablespoons butter
50 grams/ 2-3 tablespoons of canola/ sunflower or rapeseed oil
30 grams/ 2 tablespoons red currant or cranberry jam
20 grams/ ½ cup fresh parsley, chopped

You will need both a large sauté pan and a large heavy bottom pot for this recipe.

- Place a large heavy bottomed pot onto your hob/stovetop on medium heat and add 1 knob/tablespoon of butter

- Add diced onion, carrot, mushroom and sauté for 5-7 minutes until softened

- Add garlic, beef bouillon, water, tomato puree, bay leaves, dried herbs

- On a large plate mix together the flour and black pepper

- In a large sauté pan heat 15 ml/ 1 tablespoon of canola or sunflower oil

- Working in batches coat the beef cubes in the seasoned flour and brown on high heat in the cooking oil

- Once the cubes are well browned but not cooked through, transfer them to the large pot and deglaze the pan with the red wine if necessary before beginning the next batch

- Once all the meat has been browned and added to the large pot, bring to the boil and then reduce heat to a very low simmer with the lid partially on for 4 hours

- Periodically, stir the stew making sure to scrape the bottom of the pot to prevent sticking

- When the meat is fall apart tender and the sauce reduced to a thick dark brown, stir in the red current jam

- Garnish with a fresh chopped parsley and a small dab of the red current jam

January

_—_

March

Hogmany
27th December
- 2nd January

Happy New Year!

My beef stew brings all the luck to the door…

The Ba is Thrown Up at 1:00 from the steps of St Magnus by Sandy McConnachie on the 25th Anniversary of his win of the Boys Ba.

Kirkwall Ba' Game

1st January

One of the longest standing traditions of the New Year is the Ba' Games of Kirkwall in Orkney. Played on both Christmas Day and New Year's Day each year, these are the last examples of what had been common Yuletide massed ba' games. This one dates back for 300 years but legend takes it back right to the time of the Earls of Orkney over 800 years ago as documented in the Orkneyinga Sagas.

Whatever the origin, you really (and I mean really) have to go and see this to believe it!

The mob is divided into two teams called the Uppies if your were born "Up the Gate" or the Doonies if you were born "Doon from the Gate". Well over 300 men gather together to play this no rules, free for all of a game through the centre of Kirkwall, which has all been safely boarded up for the event. There is only a single point scored in the game: the Uppies must bounce the Ba' off the wall of their goal (a house that now stands where the orginal gates of the town once did), and the Doonies must get it into the water of the town's harbour which is about a mile wide.

January – March

Kirkwall Ba' Game
1st January

Preparing for the Ba'

Steaming in...

The Ba' is handmade by a local cobbler each year and paid for (approximately £100) by the person honoured to begin the game with the "Throw Up" from the steps of St Magnus Cathedral. This is usually a former winner of the Ba' or one of their family members.

For the next say six to nine hours the steaming, heaving mass of men roll through the streets, pausing in great groaning scrums, only to occasionally break out if the Ba' is in play. The crowd of hundreds hug the scrum tightly but always remain aware and on their toes ready to hoof it if necessary.

There are no rules, no officials, no police, and no barricades to protect the crowds – and this is part of what makes it one of the single most exciting experiences of my life. To be in a slow moving throng with tensions sky-high, surrounded by the deepest most thrilling sound of the rumble of a thousand feet moving in a single mass with the possibility of them exploding in any direction at any time is exhilarating. When you add in the explosive shouting of a four foot high white-haired granny next to you barking "C'mon Uppies" it is more than enough to get your heart jumping!

After eight long but thrilling hours of this, the Doonies scored by wetting the Ba' in the harbour. But the action does not stop there. As the Ba' itself is the trophy, once one of the teams has won, several members of that

January

–

March

Kirkwall Ba' Game
1st January

same team then turn on each other to try to garner the Ba' itself to be the player to win the Ba'. So, the very folk that have been struggling together all day, then turn and set upon each other in an almighty struggle, in this case in the North Sea at night in January, *for about another hour*, until at last one emerges with the Ba' held over his head. Herculean effort does not describe it.

There are boys Ba' Games on both Christmas and New Year's as well but they are much more running based games than the men's. Yes, there was a Women's Ba' Game held once in 1945/46 but the townspeople were horrified at the level of violence and have abolished it ever since!

Staying in Orkney for the New Year with the best hospitality for the most exciting sporting event ever, was an honour and privilege.

I am not likely to forget it – ever.

The Doonies battling for the
Ba' in Kirkwall Harbour

Ba' Game Patties

Serves 8

The day before the Ba' Game my wonderful hostess Susan took me to the local chip shop in Kirkwall for my introduction to the Orkney wonder of Patties. Pronounced Pa-Tay, it is the touch stone food for returning locals to feel at home, and an absolute must for visitors. If you can envision a fish cake that has been rolled in breadcrumbs, battered and fried and then simply substitute a peppery savoury beef instead of the fish you will have some idea of what a Pattie might be like. Why they are not just called 'beef cakes' I do not know, but to my mind that would make more sense, and help convey the overall manliness of the participants of the Ba' Game!

On the day of the Ba' itself, the action was so exciting that I didn't leave for one second. Not a sip of tea or a morsel of food passed my lips as I was transfixed by the action. However, as the sun went down and the January chill set in, I was desperately hoping for an enterprising soul to bring me a newspaper cone filled with steaming chips and bite sized patties – my remembered craving from the day before. As such, I have conjured up my wish so that you too can enjoy a taste of Orkney while keeping nimble of foot. Not just for eating at the Ba' Game, these can be savoured at any outdoor sporting event.

For the Patties:

800 grams/ 2 lbs potatoes diced and boiled for 20 minutes then mashed (leftovers are OK)
500 grams/ 1 lb minced/ ground beef
1 large onion, diced
Salt & Black Pepper to taste
7 ml/ 1 teaspoon Worcestershire sauce
15 ml/ 1 tablespoon Brown Sauce or Ketchup
100 grams crumb coating (Ruskoline)

January
—
March

Kirkwall Ba' Game
1st January

For the Batter:

500 grams/ 2 cups plain flour
7 ml/ 1 teaspoon salt
1 bottle/ 12 oz or 300 ml beer or sparkling water
1 quart/ 1 litre light oil for frying

- Set a large pot on the hob/ stovetop and add the oil – heat to 200 C/ 400 F

- In a large fry pan (dry) add the diced onions and the minced/ground beef. Sauté 5-7 minutes
- When the onions are translucent and the beef is well browned, add the Worcester sauce, brown sauce (or ketchup) and stir for 2-3 more minutes

- Salt & Pepper to taste, remove from heat and set aside

- Cook and mash the potatoes

- Add the beef mix to the potatoes and mix well, leave to cool

- On a large plate spread the crumb coating (Ruskoline)

- Scoop a heaped teaspoon of the pattie mix and drop onto the crumb, and roll into a ball

- Once all of the mix has been rolled and crumbed, set aside and mix up the batter

- When the oil is hot, gently drop the crumbed pattie balls into the batter coating gently with two forks

- Lift out of the batter and drop into the hot oil for 3-4 minutes or until golden brown

- Working in batches so the temperature of the oil doesn't drop, once the pattie balls are done remove them from the oil and drain on kitchen roll/ paper towel

- Serve 6-8 balls per person or 5 if serving with chips/ fries

January

—

March

Kirkwall Ba' Game
1st January

17

My Orcadian
wish fulfilment

The Burning Of The Clavie

As a child raised on stories of Rip Van Winkle and the Legend of Sleepy Hollow, it will come as no surprise that I have a fertile imagination.

I have always been drawn to Celtic notions of slipping away to join mysterious midnight parties that may last an hour or a year, depending on your fate.

So, when on my very first visit to Scotland, I stood on a windy promontory that jutted into the Moray Firth, and was told of the local fire festival – so old that its origins are lost in the mists of time.

I was transported into another world.

The Burning of the Clavie is an ancient fire festival held in the small fishing village of Burghead in the North East of Scotland, on the 11th of January each year, thus maintaining the date of the Julian New Year. Preparations for the festival begin with a large wooden-stave barrel being cut in half and nailed to a long handled pole. The term Clavie is attributed both to the Latin **clavis** for nail and to **claibh**, the Gaelic word for basket or creel. My bet is on the Gaelic. The barrel is filled with tar and several other staves and set alight, before being paraded through the village by the Clavie King. The main streets are thronged with people, but just as many beat a quick path down through the narrow cobbled alleyways of the village to get a good

January
—
March

The Burning
of the Clavie

19

The Burning of the
Clavie at Burghhead

The Clavie being carried
through the streets

position to view the Clavie's final destination: a permanent stone structure built on top of Doorie Hill, the remnants of an ancient Pictish Fort.

The fire is fed by a spectacular amount of flammable liquid and more staves are added to the bonfire. As the wood burns, pieces are hauled out and thrown down the hill towards the crowd of several hundred gathered in the cold night. A flimsy fence proves no match to keep the people away from scrambling onto the hill to gather their glowing embers. Traditionally, the embers were taken into the homes to re-ignite the fires for the New Year and then to be placed up the chimney to ward off witches.

I went after my piece like most of my peers would go after Manolo Blahniks on sale, and melted gloves aside...

I got my bit of the Clavie!

The Aftermath of the Clavie
looking out over Moray Firth

January
—
March

The Burning
of the Clavie

Smoked Haddock Chowder

Serves 4 - 6

After enjoying the spectacle of the Burning of the Clavie, your immediate thoughts turn to the very strong desire to re-warm yourself. As you and the rest of the crowd have been thoroughly saturated with the perfume of the billowing smoke you can't help but crave the local speciality of smoked haddock chowder, better known within Scotland as Cullen Skink.

Cullen is another fishing village just a few stops down the coast from Burghhead and the unfortunate sounding word Skink comes from a medieval catch-all term for soup (literally the shinbone of an animal that was used to make broth). Regardless, it so simple yet so divine and the perfect winter warmer for all occasions!

For the Soup

2 cups/ 500 ml milk
500 grams/ ½ lb undyed smoked haddock (any smoked whitefish will do)
15 g/ 1 tablespoon butter
1 medium onion, diced fine
1 leek, washed and diced fine
4 medium potatoes, diced large
1 bay leaf
Spring onions to garnish

January

—

March

The Burning
of the Clavie

- In a large pan place the fish fillets and cover with milk – add bay leaf

- Warm to gentle simmer for 3-5 minutes but do not boil

- Lift fish out of the milk and set aside

- In another pan, melt butter and sauté onions and leek for 5-7 minutes on low heat

- Add diced potatoes and add cooking milk from the fish. Simmer until potatoes are tender

- Remove any skin or bones from cooled haddock and break into flakes (reserve some for garnish)

- Add the remaining fish to the soup and discard the bay leaf

- Mash up the soup with a fork until thick but elements are still visible

- Serve garnished with reserved flakes and chopped spring onions – heaven!

When in Rome baby...

First cast of the season

Opening
of the Salmon
Season

- Mid January

Salmon is incredibly important for Scotland, both as a signature food and also because its reputation and abundance makes Scotland a destination for world-class sport fishing. The opening season for this "King of Fish" has been celebrated in an annual ceremony at the Kenmore Hotel in Perthshire since 1947. The town of Kenmore is situated at the juncture of where Loch Tay becomes the River Tay and has long been held as

one of the very best spots in Scotland for salmon fishing.

Each year on a chilly January morning, locals, invited dignitaries and fisherman from all over Scotland gather outside the Kenmore Hotel for bacon rolls and drams of whisky provided by Dewars the local whisky distillery. Welcomes and blessings are made and then the crowds, led by the **Vale of Atholl Junior Pipe Band**, make their way down to the riverside where the first boat is blessed with whisky before it sets out into the water. Huge cheers of "Tight Lines" go up as the fisherman in the boat make their first cast and then the other anglers get their rods into the air to begin yet another season of salmon fishing in Scotland. The proceeds from the fishing permits sold on the opening day go to charity and the prize for the biggest catch of the day from anywhere on the River Tay is the **McTaggart Kenmore Trophy** and *a gallon* of **Dewars** whisky!

January — March

Opening of the
Salmon Season
Mid-January

25

Vale of Atholl
Junior Pipe Band

Former Provost blessing the
boat of the season with whisky

LOCH TAY BOATING CENTRE

Aside from having to leave your bed whilst it is still dark and brave the A9 in the snow, the overall ceremony is pure magic.

Like so many of the events that mark the calendar in Scotland, whether large or small there is a mix of intimate and majestic all rolled into one. Salmon, and all of fishing in Scotland, is as important today as it has been for centuries and with careful and respectful protection and management it will be for centuries to come.

There is also a closing ceremony in October as the salmon season draws to a close. As everyone gathers at dusk, an incredibly brave and co-ordinated piper stands upright in the boat and is rowed under the iconic Kenmore Bridge to the waiting platform at the hotel. A fireworks display delights all as the season is officially brought to a close.

Good Luck Nip
Courtesy of Dewars Whisky

January
—
March

Opening of the
Salmon Season
Mid-January

Campfire Breakfast Boats

– Serves 4

As we stood outside the Kenmore Hotel with the snow swirling around us at a very early hour of the morning, I was very impressed by how hearty the anglers were to brave the elements on this bright but freezing day. Outside the hotel, bacon rolls were served on large trays to those anglers lucky enough to attend the event, but what of all of the other fishermen who weren't here to enjoy them?

My thoughts turned to how to create a warming and sustaining breakfast for those crazy enough to have camped out to secure their fishing space along the river. And since the major part of the Opening of the Salmon Season ceremony is to bless the first boat of the season, voila! – the breakfast boat was born. The potatoes can be baked in a campfire wrapped in foil from the night before or even brought along ready for stuffing!

For the Breakfast Boats

4 medium potatoes, baked at 180 C/ 350 F for 1 hour or foil-wrapped & baked in a campfire for 1 hour
4 slices of smoked bacon, cooked and diced
4 medium eggs
250 g / 1 cup shredded cheese
Salt & Pepper

- Once the potatoes are cooked and cooled, take a spoon and gently scoop out the inside leaving a good thickness so the potato can still hold its shape

- (Save the scooped potato for a quick way to make fish cakes later in the day with your catch)

*January
–
March*

Hogmany
27th December
- 2nd January

- Fry the bacon until crisp and break up into small bits

- Lightly salt and pepper the inside of each potato boat, and add grated cheese and bacon to each

- Crack one egg into each boat and top with any remaining cheese

- Cover and bake in a 180 C/ 350 F oven or re-wrap in foil and return to camp fire coals for 20 minutes

- Let cool slightly, pick up & enjoy

A hot, hearty start to a very chilly day...

Burn's Night

Burn's Night or a **Burn's Supper** is held on the 25th of January to honour Scotland's National Poet, Robert Burns (1759 –1796). The famed son of a ploughman: his works and reputation as a champion of the common man have been celebrated around the globe since his own lifetime in the 18th century. A Burn's Night can be a small gathering or a huge formal affair.

All events endeavour to embrace the spirit and works of Burns, with copious lashings of haggis, whisky and entertainment.

January
—
March

Burn's Night
25th January

30

The basic format is the same and works on a variety of scales. The guests are warmly welcomed, followed by Burn's *Selkirk Grace*. After the Grace follows the ceremonial piping in of the Haggis with a robust reading of the illustrious *Address to a Haggis*, which climaxes in the reader plunging his dirk (knife) into the steaming dish for full dramatic effect. Whilst the guests enjoy their meal of Haggis, Neeps & Tatties (haggis, mashed turnips and mashed potatoes), readings and toasts by the Bard abound, most usually *Tam O' Shanter*. Performances of Highland Dance or even a full Ceilidh may follow for a most merry evening. As the company, the meal and the poetry cast their warm spell – particularly welcome on a dark and cold January night – things finish with a group rendition of Burn's most well-known song *Auld Lang Syne*.

The first Burn's Night was held on 29th January in 1802 by the first ever Burn's Club, the date on which they believed was his birthday. Parish records later confirmed that his birthday was actually the 25th of January and Burn's Nights have been celebrated all around the globe, particularly by the Scottish diaspora, ever since.

Whether you are a fan of Burn's, poetry in general, Scottish culture or not, I can highly recommend the hearty experience of a Burn's Night. As far as gatherings go, it is actually very easy to host one and a great excuse to bring a wide variety of friends together, as there is something for everyone!

Selkirk Grace

Some hae meat and canna eat,
And some wad eat that want it,
But we hae meat and we can eat,
Sae let the Lord be thankit.

Sláinte!

('Cheers' in Gaelic)

January
—
March

Burn's Night
25th January

31

Haggis, Neeps & Tattie Pie

– Serves 8-12

Burn's Night is far too much fun for anyone to be stuck in the kitchen. As such, my game plan for a foolproof evening is this: a huge array of platters of self-serve canapés (hors d'oeuvres), this make-ahead Haggis Pie, and invite one of your guests to provide a traditional trifle (also known as a Tipsy Laird due to the large amount of whisky!).

This pie serves several purposes in that it incorporates all the main components of the meal and it couldn't be easier to heat and serve, no matter how wild things get! Although I am now fully converted and love the taste of haggis, I can remember how daunted I felt when I was of the uninitiated and presented with my first plate of haggis. Somehow, this pie makes the whole thing less daunting and much less formal. Sit back and enjoy the company, the poetry, the dancing and music for a truly wonderful evening. If haggis just really isn't your thing, any spiced beef or lamb will do.

For the Pie:

900 g Haggis/Vegetarian Haggis (2x 450g)
1 large swede/turnip/rutabaga – about 500-600 g/ 1 lb
1 kilo/ 2 lbs potatoes, diced
50 grams/ 1 cup grated cheese
60 grams/ 4 tablespoons butter – divided

For the Sauce – optional:

1 jar of orange marmalade
50 ml/ ¼ cup whisky
30 grams/ 2 tablespoon butter

- Set three large pots on the hob/stovetop

- Place the two haggis in one and cover with water. Boil for 1 hour

- Place the diced potatoes in a second pot and cover with salted water, boil until fork tender, about ½ hour

- In the third pot, place the peeled and diced swede and cover with water, boil until tender, about ½ hour

- When all three component have been cooked, drained and mashed in their separate pots – allow to cool

- Once cooled, in a large casserole/ pie dish layer the haggis, then the swede and top with the mashed potatoes. Cover with grated cheese

- If making ahead place in fridge

- To bake the pie, preheat an oven to 200 C or 400 F and bake for roughly 45-60 minutes

- When the pie is almost finished place the ingredients for the sauce in a pan and heat for 5 minutes stirring often. Serve in a small jug on the side of the pie

An easy and delicious way to embrace the flavours of Burn's Night...

The Galley aflame

34

Up Helly Aa

Last Tuesday of January

Up Helly Aa is the winter festival held on the last Tuesday of January in Lerwick, Shetland, marking what had been the end of Old Yule in the Julian Calender.

The largest Fire Festival in Europe, it is a 24 hour celebration that is as multi-layered as it is fun.

The modern event is a bewildering combination of ancient New Year traditions, medieval guising, 19th century Temperance movements and a rising awareness of the Nordic heritage of the islands. So what had began as some raucous lads dragging burning tar barrels through the streets (an act that was attempted to be outlawed in 1874 for causing too much damage), has been reinterpreted into a torchlight procession with a Viking Longboat (complete with dragon's head), music, song and performances by over forty squads of men: creating a truly spectacular event.

Each year a "Guiser Jarl" is chosen to lead the celebrations. The term Jarl mean Earl or Chieftain and Guiser is the term applied to anyone in disguise (even for children at Halloween). He and his Jarl Squad are the centrepiece of the day and the only ones dressed as Vikings. The day begins with the unveiling of the "Bill", a painted placard with plenty of tongue in cheek and even off-colour jokes from the local community. The Brass Band sounds and the daytime parade begins, with first the boys' Jarl Squad and then the men's Jarl Squad in full custom-made Viking regalia. Following the parade and placard, the Jarl Squads make a full day of appearances in local schools, hospitals and museums until night falls and the truly extraordinary part of festival begins.

January
—
March

Up Helly Aa
Last Tuesday
of January

The Jarl Squad of Up Helly Aa' 2013

At about 7.00 p.m. the forty plus squads, led by the Jarl Squad assemble below the Town Hall and all the town's lights are extinguished. A "maroon" (a mortar-launched flare) is fired and the torches are lit with additional flares. The red light blooms against the smoke-filled blackness and the whiff of burning parrafin all create an other worldly spectacle, which is then taken to the surreal as a big brass band kicks in to lead the torchlight procession of between 800-1000 men through the town. With the winter wind whipping them on, the procession snakes through Lerwick until entering a park where the flaming circle of men toss their torches onto the handcrafted longboat. Singing loudly, they gather around the burning ship until the dragon's head falls off.

The magnificent parades, torchlight procession and the burning of the handcrafted Viking Galley are an unbelievable sight to behold. But this is just the public part of the celebration that most tourists see. For the Shetlanders themselves, this event is just the beginning of the true celebrations that take place in the twenty-six Community Halls that are spread throughout Lerwick. This is when everyone heads off to one of the many halls for a rotating twelve hour party of traditional music, and wild performances by the dozens of squads.

The Jarl Squad remain in their Viking regalia, all the others are in costumes relevant to their squad's themed routines that they must perform at each Hall throughout the night. These will be directly pertaining to Island life or events of the past year. The squads rotate to all the halls in a cyclical shedule, but the Jarl Squad travels to the same halls in the opposite direction, trumping any other squad's performance upon arrival. At each hall large groups of people gather, with dance bands and a group of hostesses serving food and refreshments to keep eveyone going all night.

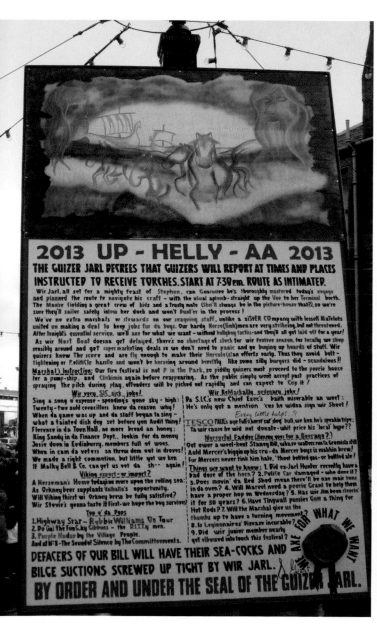

The Bill

Junior Jarl Squad

The Guizer Jarl, Stephen Grant, at the Helm of the Galley

A Member of the Jarl Squad, Andrew Aitken in full regalia

The squads perform their routines at all the halls all night long being sure to keep their faces covered throughout the dancing. Despite the heavy drinking that ensues you must be able to manage all twenty-six performances and not disgrace yourself or your squad as a result.

So again, if you are up for a twenty-four hours of parades, music, dancing, performances and all round fabulousness...

I suggest that you put

Up Helly Aa

on your bucket list!

January
–
March

Up Helly Aa
Last Tuesday
of January

Reestit Mutton Soup

What is actually served at the halls for Up Helly Aa' is a Shetland speciality called Reestit (meaning rested or cured) Mutton Soup with soft bannock sandwiches of corned beef. When I enquired as to why those foods in particular, the answer seemed to be, "Well, that was what was available at that time of year."

It is made by boiling a salted mutton joint in water and then pouring the water off. After adding fresh water you add diced onion, potato, turnips, (carrots can be added but are controversial), and boil until the vegetables are soft. The meat is diced and added back in upon serving. It is rich, hearty and super salty but really hits the spot to revive you in the circumstances.

Sadly, unless you are up for brining your mutton in a barrel for a month and then hanging it to smoke over a peat fire for several more, Reestit Mutton is very hard to find other than from Shetland butchers. In a pinch, corned beef could be used as a substitute.

January
–
March

Up Helly Aa
Last Tuesday
of January

39

Yule Board –

A Selection of Cured Meats & Fish, With Pickles, Chutneys, Oatcakes & Bannocks

Serves 8

When I come inside from being lashed by freezing rain (as I was repeatedly during Up Helly Aa), I look for something warm and hearty to return feeling to my extremities. But as a host I also want something easy that can be put on a buffet so people can help themselves and to fuel the night's festivities.

However, the spirit of both the location and event can be embraced by continuing the Nordic influences of a Yule Board or (Jule Board). It is a variation of a Smorgasbord, consisting of cured, salted and smoked meats, fish, hearty vegetables, and pots of pickles, chutney and jams to set off their flavours. For the Up Helly Aa Yule Board I selected, Pastrami (smoked corned beef), Crowdie (a fresh sharp cheese), and a Scottish blue cheese with oatcakes and whisky marmalade, in addition to Smoked Salmon, Mackeral, potatoes and pickled fennel with soft bannocks.

All of these salty foods will require enormous amounts of liquids to compensate, so be prepared and let the all night party begin!

January
—
March

Up Helly Aa
Last Tuesday
of January

40

A delicious & sustaining feast!

Up Helly Aa
Last Tuesday
of January

The start

A Shop front with custom made Ba' game boarding

The girls

Jedburgh Callants Ba' Game

Thursday after Shrove Tuesday, February

The town of Jedburgh (Jedhart to the locals) was founded in the 9th Century, and is one of five of the Scottish Border towns that still celebrate an ancient Shrove Tuesday or "Fastern's E'en" game of "Handba" or "Ba' Game" of the Uppies versus the Doonies. Whilst these no-rules open games once filled the length and breadth of Medieval Britain, only fifteen games remain today, each with their own variations. The Ba' in Jedburgh is a small hand held leather ball with ribbons decorating the top.

This leather "Ba" is a much more humane alternative to the earlier "Ba's" which were heads of slaughtered enemies.

Once the ba is "hailed" or scored the ribbons are detached and redeemed for prize money or a a sponsored gift such as a round of drinks at a pub.

January – March

Jedburgh Callants
Ba' Game
Thursday after
Shrove Tuesday,
February

A ba dedicated to the memory of her son.

Billy Gillies – The (unoffical) "Man"

The boys' game or 'Callants Game' begins at noon and is largely defined by the incredible amount of running around trying to smuggle the ball to the goals at opposite ends of the very steep and long High Street. Large crowds gather to watch the various throws that begin play. The exuberence and energy are palpable and whilst all play can disappear from view for a good length of time, any spectators need to be on their toes as a running, rumbling herd of fifty to sixty young boys can engulf you in play if you are not careful. The town's shops all close for the day and are boarded up to protect their precious window fronts.

The men's game gets underway at 2.00 pm and runs concurrent to the boys' game. However, the men spend almost all their time in a slow moving scrum, that only occasionally bursts apart, while the swirl of the boys' game often flows through and around the more stationary heap of men. Both games go on for hours, with the men's usually ending at about 9.00 pm at night.

Both games were traditionally held on the day before lent or Shrove Tuesday but now tend to fall on the second week of February (usually on St Valentine's Day as the girls of the town complain).

This is an all day endurance in the chill of late winter that will get the blood pumping for all who view or play the game.

As this is an all-day outdoor event, both players and spectators alike need to be suitably sustained throughout the game. Traditionally played on Shrove Tuesday or Pancake Day, this was a great feast day when you were to clear out your stores of all things yummy to prepare for the lean days of Lent.

A rare sight of the ba' in play!

Raspberry Filled Handcakes with Easy Maple Frosting

Makes 12

My biggest challenge with Pancake Day is that making a (not very portable) hot sticky breakfast, on what is usually a school day doesn't work well for me. Additionally, I personally prefer my sweets in the afternoon with coffee or tea rather than first thing in the morning. As such, I have re-interpreted the traditional pancake into the much handier cupcake or 'handcakes' as I prefer, filled with local strawberry jam and topped with easy Maple Frosting to embrace the richness required of a traditional feast day. This should keep players and spectators going through the long afternoon of events!

For the Handcake Ingredients:

350 grams/ 2 cups/ 9 oz plain flour
10 grams/ 1 ½ teaspoons baking powder
2 grams/ ½ teaspoon baking (bicarb) soda
1 gram/ ½ teaspoon salt
60 grams/ 4 tablespoon sugar
250 ml/ 250 grams/ 1 cup buttermilk
2 eggs
50 grams/ 4 tablespoons butter
15 grams/ 1 tablespoon Maple Syrup
Raspberry or Strawberry Jam for filling
Maple Frosting – recipe follows
Golden or Maple Syrup for drizzling

Easy Maple Frosting

400 g/ 16 oz softened cream cheese (Philadelphia)
45 grams/ 45 ml/ 3 tablespoons thick Maple Syrup

January
–
March

Jedburgh Callants
Ba' Game
Thursday after
Shrove Tuesday,
February

46

A portable way to enjoy
Pancake Day!

- Preheat oven to 180 C/ 350 F and line a medium muffin tin with paper cases

- Preheat an oven to 180 C / 350 F

- Place paper liners in a muffin tin

- In a large bowl add the dry ingredients for the handcakes

- Fill the muffin cases approximately 2/3 full with the batter

- Bake for 20 - 30 minutes depending on size of muffin cases

- While the handcakes are baking, place ingredients for Maple Frosting in a bowl and mix thoroughly

- Once handcakes are cooled, fill each cake with a small amount of strawberry jam, either by filling from the underside with a pastry bag, or using an apple corer (or teaspoon) to cut a small piece of the top of the cake to spoon in jam

- Top with frosting and fresh raspberries, and for extra decadence a drizzle of syrup

January

—

March

Jedburgh Callants
Ba' Game
Thursday after
Shrove Tuesday,
February

Winter's End

In traditional Celtic lore the end of the winter months were welcomed with the coming of the goddess Bride, later known as St. Bridget. Her feast day was known as Imbolc (meaning 'in the belly' to herald the start of calving season) and is usually recognised to be February the 1st or 2nd. In some versions of mythology she comes and dips her toe into a stream to return warmth and banish the winter chill, and in some she washed a great tartan (plaid) shawl in the water for three stormy days until calm is restored and the tartan is pure white.

Bridgit was known as the goddess of poetry, iron and silver work, healing, marriage and childbirth. As one researcher stated, "she was the Mary and the Juno to the Celt". As Christianity absorbed the ancient customs and characters into its liturgy, Bridget was also associated with Mary, mother of Jesus and the feast day became Candlemas.

Regardless of one's belief system this point in the calendar is set between the vernal and spring equinox, so from this point onwards the days get noticeably lighter and you may even start to see snowdrops and a few brave crocuses poke their noses from the damp soil. While the blushes of spring are undeniable, nobody is coming close to putting away the winter coats for a while yet.

However, winter is officially over and even if the weather doesn't play along there are many other events that begin at this time. Namely this is the season for the Scottish Six Nations Rugby Tournament and also the start of the Scottish Grande National Horserace, so there are plenty of ways to entertain yourself until things warm up a bit.

St. Bridget's Church, Dalgety Bay, Fife.
Dating back to at least 1178

January – March

The May Queen (Beltane)

April
–
June

The welcome colours of Spring!

Easter (Pasch)

Easter is celebrated in Scotland much as it has been for centuries. The joyous welcoming of spring, and of course now, the certain promise of chocolate, brings merriment to all. Traditionally, Easter was known as **Pasch** with its roots in the Hebrew word *pesach*, meaning Passover.

On Easter many different customs surrounding eggs, whether decorating, hunting and most commonly rolling down a hill, reign supreme. There are endless chocolate eggs, bunnies and chicks given to children and many families gather together for the festive day.

Easter originates from pre-Christian times when offerings were made to the goddess of spring Eastre or Orstara, whose symbol was a rabbit or hare. As Christianity spread across Europe, under the guidance of Pope Gregory in the 6th century, the clergy was encouraged to assimilate people's existing pagan beliefs and customs but re-interpret them into the fold of Christianity.

Food is a huge part of any Easter celebration

As the fresh new shoots of green have returned and the land is awash with nature renewing itself. It is not all just chocolate and sweets for the children!

Easter in my parents' house was a very big deal. My mother would usually bake a huge ham served with scalloped potatoes (dauphinoise), and a beautiful spinach salad. As a family we were strongly encouraged to observe Lent and as such every year my father would give up his evening glass of wine and my mother would give up her beloved instant coffee. We were all glad to see Easter morning!

Asparagus and Spring Onion Quiche

Serves 8-12

Even though I enjoy roasts of all kinds, there is something about being surrounded by frolicking baby lambs and fluffy chicks that steers me toward a vegetarian feast on Easter. I like to hold true to the almighty egg as a symbol of rebirth and renewal, and the fresh green vegetable are a welcome sign that winter is truly over.

A 25 cm/ 10 inch pie shell works best for this delicate but flavourful dish. I like to serve this with a spinach salad as a special nod to my mother.

For the Crust:

350 grams/ 2 cups plain flour
2 grams/ ½ teaspoon salt
150 ml/ ½ cup canola or sunflower oil
75 ml/ ¼ cup milk
Mix wet ingredients into flour
Mix well until dough comes together
Dump dough into a greased pie dish and press into shape with your fingers
Prick several times with a fork and bake at 200 C/ 400 F for 10 minutes

For the Quiche:

500 grams/ 1 lb asparagus lightly steamed
2 spring onions/ scallions, finely chopped
6 medium eggs
250 grams/ ½ lb cottage cheese
120 grams/ 1 cup shredded cheddar cheese
5 ml/ 1 teaspoon Herbs de Provence
2.5 ml/ ½ teaspoon baking powder

- Steam asparagus and set aside

- Mix the remaining ingredients together and pour into pie shell

- Lay the asparagus spears in a circular pattern on top of the egg mixture.

- Bake at 180 C/ 350 F for 45 - 60 minutes until set in the middle

A fresh way to enjoy the beautiful vegetables of springtime.

The Treaty of Arbroath

The Treaty of Arbroath is one of the seminal documents of Scottish History: signed on the 6th of April 1320 at Arbroath Abbey by fifty-one dignitaries and members of the Scottish Nobility, the document declared Scotland an independent sovereign state that had the right to use force to defend itself. Created in the form of a letter to the then Pope John XXII in Avignon, the document states several points of significant importance. Firstly, that Scotland was and always had been independent (longer even than had England) and that the independence of Scotland was held to be with the people of the nation rather than the King. This radical concept of "popular sovereignty" stated that the Nobility only existed by the will of the people and could be altered as such, rather than by the then prevailing concept of a divine appointment by royalty.

The Pope heeded the declarations within the document and in response issued six Papal Bulls (Papal Bulls were a form of public communication issued by Popes during times of great importance) favouring Scotland's claims. The document itself is indeed inspiring, with the most quoted passage stating:

> "... for, as long as but a hundred of us remain alive, never will we on any conditions be brought under English rule. It is in truth not glory, nor riches, nor honours that we are fighting, but freedom – for that alone, which no honest man gives up but with life itself."

The majestic ruins of Arbroath Abbey

This document not only plays a huge part in Scottish History, but has become the foundation for several other documents in the following centuries, not the least of which is the Declaration of Independence for the United States of America in 1776.

The Treaty is presented by the Bishop

The Declaring of
Support by Nobililty

The Treaty of Arbroath is believed to have been drafted by Bernard of Kilwinnning who was the Chancellor of Scotland and the Abbot of Arbroath. Arbroath Abbey itself was founded in 1178 by King William the Lion and a group of Benedictine monks from Kelso Abbey in the Scottish Borders. Dedicated to St Thomas Becket, the Abbey has been the setting not only for the Treaty of Arbroath but also the return of the Stone of Destiny in April 1951. Each year since 1947, the Arbroath Abbey Timethemes group perform a magnificent re-enactment of the signing of what many see as the foundation document for Scottish Sovereignty.

Arbroath Smokie Pate with Oatcakes and Chutney

Serves 2

The name Arbroath triggers two things – the Treaty of Arbroath and Arbroath Smokies. What better way to celebrate a place of such singular and ancient prestige than to embrace them both in a single event? Arbroath Smokies are hot smoked haddock that are just beyond sublime. Aside from hot and fresh out of the smoking cask, this is my second favourite way to enjoy the exquisite flavour and toast the historical importance of Arbroath.

For the Pate:

200 grams/ 1 cup/ 1 small tub Philadelphia cream cheese
100 grams/ 2-3 cooked fillets of smoked haddock/ Arbroath Smokies
10 grams/ ¾ tablespoon horseradish sauce
¼ teaspoon cracked black pepper (no salt)

- Mix the soft cheese, horseradish and pepper together

- Flake the haddock into the mix and blend well with a fork

- Serve with oatcakes, biscuits or crackers

- Apricot and/or mango chutney work well with the smoky pate

Ancient, soulful and all round wonderful, Arbroath is a treasure of the past and present!

A rich and smoky treat to
savour this local delicacy!

April
–
June

The Treaty
of Arbroath
6th April

61

Beltane

Evening of 30th April

As springtime comes to Scotland in the form of the blooming of the Hawthorn (or May) flowers, those in the know begin to ready for the all-night party known as Beltane. One of the ancient Celtic fire festivals, Beltane is a time of clearing out the cobwebs, asking for blessings for the coming growing season, but most of all just a chance to party.

Set atop Calton Hill in Edinburgh, Beltane is a spectacular piece of outdoor theatre that processes to several locations re-enacting the marriage of the Green Man and the May Queen. Carried out as a parade of drums, fire bearers, red dervishes, blue dancers and white ladies; it is an impressive and exciting spectacle to behold.

What started out as a free community event is now a sell-out event attended by some 12,000 people.

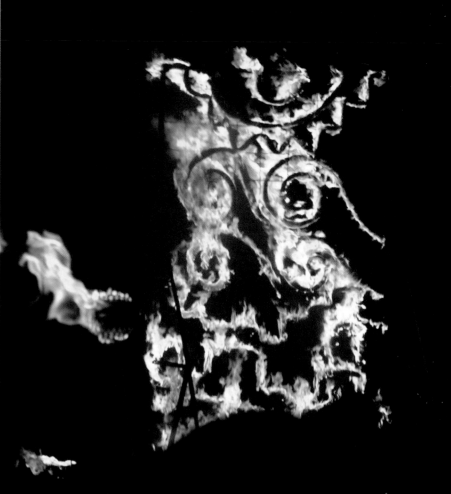

I also hear from very reliable sources that it is not quite as wild (or completely naked) as it was in the early days of the festival. Before its current location, the early events were set upon Arthur's Seat. This modern interpretation of the festival began in 1988, and was created by musicians, artists, and folklorists not just as a celebration of culture but also a protest of the then Thatcher government's restrictions on the right to gather in public spaces.

If you can't get to Edinburgh you can have your own Beltane celebration wherever you live. The basic themes are of "out with the old and in with the new", a hope for prosperity, for good luck and of blowing off steam after the winter months. The colours of Beltane are red and white, and a good amount of green for the Green Man himself. Light a fire or candle at sunset and try to (safely) keep it going until dawn when your night of unabashed merriment should end with the washing of your face in the fresh dew of May Day.

If you happen to be face down in said grass by them, well two birds/one stone I guess.

For those of a more decorous manner, a backyard BBQ with friends is the perfect way to herald Beltane. Be sure to gather lots of flowers for decoration and the women should feel free to pop a few fresh buds into their hair. The menu should reflect the wildness of the original event so this is the time to break out the wild salmon and maybe some venison. One of the main traditions of Beltane festivities gone by would be to drive the cattle between two fires as a blessing, so maybe not so much with the beef for this occasion. You can also gather the welcome fresh bounty of springtime with asparagus, spinach and off course our spectacular strawberries.

April
—
June

Beltane
Evening of
30th April

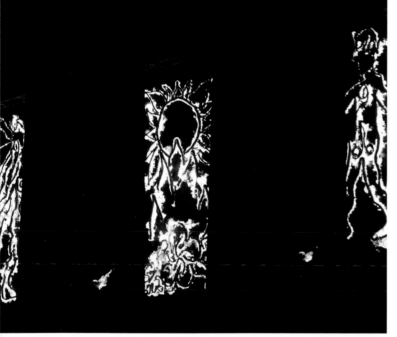

Beltane Salmon on a Plank of Native Ash

Serves four

Cooking food on a plank is common in both Native American and Scandinavian traditions. It is fun, easy and imparts fantastic flavour whether you are cooking on the BBQ or in the oven. The cooking planks are easily accessible in most countries via on-line sellers or BBQ supply stores. If using your own, make sure that your wood is untreated and has no preservatives. Cedar is the most common wood used in plank cooking, but I chose Ash as it is indigenous to Scotland and for heightened Celtic symbolism in honour of Beltane. You do not need to go to such lengths but Ash is tasty I can assure you!

Ingredients

4 salmon fillets
1 plank – untreated cedar, ash or oak

For the Honey Mustard Sauce

30 ml/ 40 grams/ 2 tablespoons Heather Honey
15 ml/ 15 grams / 1 tablespoon Dijon mustard
15 ml/ 15 grams/ 1 tablespoon butter

For the Crumb Topping

50 ml/ 25 grams or 1/4 cup dried breadcrumbs
50 ml/ 25 grams or 1/4 cup chopped hazelnuts (almonds/ walnuts/ pecans work as well)
30 ml/ 10 grams/ 2 tablespoon fresh parsley, chopped

- Prepare planks according to cooking method (brush with oil for oven; soak in water for 2 hours for BBQ)

- In one small bowl mix up the Honey Mustard Sauce

- In another small bowl mix together the crumb topping

- Preheat cooking source - 200 C/400 F for oven, Medium High for BBQ

- Place salmon fillets on plank & lightly season with salt & pepper

- Spoon the Honey Mustard Sauce over fish and top with Breadcrumb Mixture

- Cook for approximately 20 minutes until fish is firm and flakes easily

Enjoy!

Gala Days

As the summer arrives in Scotland many towns and villages prepare for their summer festivals or Gala Days. The activities, dates and traditions vary from town to town but almost everywhere has a local event that can last from one day to a week-long celebration.

In the town of Dunfermline, once the ancient capital of Scotland, the annual Children's Gala was championed by its most famous son, Andrew Carnegie. Originally organised by the Dunfermline Co-Operative Society in 1902, the Gala's Organisation and Funding was sponsored by The Carnegie Trust from 1903 through to the mid-1970s. Each year a parade of local bands and children from local primary schools attired in colourful costumes, parade down the medieval high street and enter Pittencrieff Park, known locally as The Glen.

These are grand affairs and much cherished by all.

The parade ends as everyone arrives into the park for lunch, and an afternoon of games and entertainment then rounds off the event. When this event started at the turn of the 20th century, this area's main income was from mills, coal mines and farming, so an event on this scale – paid for in full – would have been a highlight of the calendar for everyone.

Gala day in Dunfermline High Street

Each year the Gala Committee and hundreds of volunteers now raise funds, and organise and host the Gala to keep the tradition alive. Last year over 3,000 primary school children took part and over 15,000 people watched the parade and entertainment in the Glen.

Kids Picnic Rolls

Serves 4

This recipe is part cheat/ part necessity. There is not a children's event in Scotland that doesn't include a) sausage rolls, b) Scotch eggs/ picnic eggs, c) Crisps/ potato chips and d) sweets or biscuits. In any one event this is fine, but by the time you hit your 5th consecutive event, you start to crave something a bit different. Every major and bargain supermarket now stacks ready-to-roll croissants (crescent rolls to you Yanks) that provide a quick, easy and slightly healthier alternative to kids picnic food. Ready rolled puff pastry works just as well.

Ingredients:

1 package ready croissants/ crescent rolls
Deli ham, cheese, turkey
Fresh seasonal fruit
Carrot sticks
1 portion local sweets or biscuits

- Preheat an oven to 180 C/ 350 F

- Open a pack of ready to roll pastry and tear along seams

- Place 1 piece of ham & cheese, turkey & cheese or just cheese in triangle.

- Roll up and place seam down on a baking tray.

- Bake for 15-20 minutes until puffed and golden.

- Let cool to room temperature.

- Pack sandwich roll in an airtight container with a variety of healthy fruits and vegetables.

*A fun family picnic
with a fresh kick!*

April
—
June

Gala Days
June &
August

Royal Highland Show – Ingliston

late June

The Royal Highland Show held at Ingliston on the outskirts of Edinburgh, is Scotland's national farming, food and rural life event. This annual event grew out of the 18th century movement for agricultural improvement, which sought to educate and update farming practice through literature and showcase events. The Royal Highland and Agricultural Society was founded in 1784 but didn't hold its first show until December of 1822 in Edinburgh's Canongate. After many decades of aristocratic support, the term Royal was officially bestowed in 1948 by King George IV, father of the current Patron, Queen Elizabeth II.

From modest beginnings the show now comprises over 5,000 head of livestock and over 180,000 attendees each year, over the four day event held in June: with displays of heavy horse, sheep shearing, wild life conservation and farrier and forging competitions. There is also a variety of shopping to enjoy in the Food & Drink Hall, craft and clothing stalls: displays of falconry, woodcarving and more than a few parades of full pipe bands add to the excitement.

This event felt very different to many of the events that I had sought out on my journey across Scotland, but the similarity with these other events was that this represented a whole world of which I was unfamiliar.

Getting up close and personal to livestock, farriers, forges and chainsaw sculpture was as exhilarating as it was exotic.

The sheer array of jobs, machines and competitive activities that were on display made me feel very much a city girl indeed, but I still enjoyed myself immensely. This year I will return with my family in tow for what I hope will become a tradition of our own.

The Royal Highland Show is not only a wonderful day out, but *THE* annual event to highlight the current as well as historical importance that the rural and agricultural communities play in Scotland.

The ubiquitous sheep

Award winners

Tweed fashions

Horsetrials,
Hounds &
Harris Tweed

Chainsaw wood carving

Rosemary & Garlic Lamb Burgers, with Feta Cheese & Lemon Mayonnaise

Serves 4

Normally, I like to make a point of not actually eating the animal being celebrated on a given event. On this occasion however, that sentiment goes out the window. For a country literally awash in sheep on every hillside, Scots eat surprisingly little lamb. The food available at the Highland Show leans heavily toward burgers and bacon rolls, so in honour of the sheep that fill our landscape, let's enjoy a real treat of a beautiful lamb burger with fresh feta cheese, red onion and summer tomato.

For the Burger Mix:

500 grams/ 1lb minced/ground lamb
1 clove, 5 ml/ 1 teaspoon fresh garlic, minced
5 ml/ 1 teaspoon dried rosemary
Salt & Pepper
4 bread rolls, split

For each Assembled Burger:

30 ml/ 2 tablespoon lemon mayo
25 grams fresh Feta cheese crumbled
½ beefsteak tomato, sliced
1/3 red onion, sliced
Cracked black pepper

- In large bowl combine minced/ ground lamb meat, garlic, dried rosemary and salt & pepper. Divide into four thin patties

- BBQ/broil/grill on high heat for 2-3 minutes per side, set aside

- While burgers are cooking, split the bread rolls and prepare vegetables

- Toast rolls open for 1-2 minutes

- Place lemon mayo on both sides of roll

- Place cooked burger on bottom roll

- Top with Feta, onion and tomato

Enjoy!

Gourmet flavours in a fairground favourite!

Summer into Spring

The transition from Spring into Summer can be quite subtle in Scotland. It is not uncommon for April to be warm and sunny and July to be very cool and wet. But it could just as easily be the other way around! It is often said that there is no wrong weather here, just the wrong clothes and the mercurial nature of what we optimistically hope to be our best months of the year embody this concept perfectly.

But rain or sunshine (or both several times in a day) that doesn't stop the landscape from being beautiful and certainly doesn't stop people from getting out and enjoying themselves.

Unlike in some countries the festivals, fairs and galas don't wait for the school year to end before they begin. It is more of a slow trickle of events turning into a flood that all are encouraged just to ride the tide.

In addition to traditional, seasonal or cultural events that arrive each year, there is also a veritable explosion of fun fairs, circuses and food markets that seem to blossom within the landscape along with the flowers.

This is a busy and beautiful time of the year and everyone knows summer has truly arrived when the new year of strawberries finally make their appearance!

April
–
June

The riders are piped across
Rennie's Bridge

July
_
September

The Jedhart Callants in the Kelso Ride

Kelso Border Ridings

– 2nd to last Saturday in July

The Border Ridings or the Common Ridings as they are also called, trace their orgins back to the 13th and 14th centuries to a time when the Border towns of Scotland had to routinely defend themselves from threats of raids, and even war from their English neighours to the South. Each town in the Borders now commemorates their heroic ancestors with a day-long ride marking the boundaries of their towns that is a highlight within each communities' summer celebrations.

Each of the Border towns elect a lead rider and attendant to host the ridings. The titles afforded these lead riders range from 'Callant' to 'Reiver' to 'Laddie' depending on the town, but each of the selected groups from each town ride not only in their own all-day event but participate in the other Border towns' rides as well, making for a full summer of riding.

Kelso's Common Riding is not as old as some, dating from only 1937, but its importance is not reduced in the least.

July
—
September

Kelso Border Ridings
2nd to last Saturday
in July

81

The riders return   Honours ceremony

The Kelsae Laddie, along with his Right Hand Man and his Left Hand Man (the Laddies from the two previous years) lead the riders into the town square and are sent on their journey with the traditional call of, "Safe Oot, Safe In". Then over two hundred riders are lead by a full pipe and drum band past the ruins of the 12th Century Kelso Abbey and over 'Rennies Bridge' that spans the River Tweed. The riders continue to the border of the neighboring town of Yetland (the home of the Gypsy King who is in the riding as well), led by the Kelso Laddies carrying the Burgh Standard. The mounted assembly then ride to the border of England, where they halt and the three principal riders cross over, gathering sprigs of fir to wear in their lapels. They then return to Yetholm town where they are treated to a lunch before climbing back onto their horses for the long ride back over the bridge again. After completing his lead on the eight hour ride, the Kelso Laddie takes off his bowler hat and accepts his offical blue bonnet. A fancy dress ball then ends the day's festivities.

Members of the town gather to see the riders off and welcome them home on their return in an impressive and evocative display, so what better way to pass the time in between than a gorgeous picnic? The elegant and flavoursome Langoustine Roll, served with Scottish Stawberries at their summertime peak and maybe a few Haggis Crips is my choice to relish this most Scottish of celebrations!

Langoustine Roll with Summer Strawberries

- Serves 2

One of the most delicious and even luxurious surprises in the edible resources of Scotland is the lovely langoustine. The *nephrops norvegicus* is a member of the lobster family but are only eight to ten centimeters (or three to six inches) in length and are also known as Norway lobster, scampi and sometimes even Dublin Bay prawns. Regardless of their moniker, they are delicious, have a taste and texture just like lobster but a touch more salty (and richer) than the larger North American version.

If you can't find langoustines fresh, the next best thing is to be cooked from frozen. However you go about preparing them, I would strongly encourage you to make this divine **Tarragon & Dijon Mayonnaise** inspired by the creator of my favourite lobster roll in Boston, Jasper White. Of course you could just use a little bit of plain mayonnaise but this is one of those strange things that is so much more than the sum of its parts – go ahead and give it a try. It is also totally fabulous on chicken, potatoes and particularly great on a ham sandwich.

After preparing the langoustines and removing them from their shells, mix a small amount of the mayo into the cooled meat. I also like to jazz things up by adding diced celery for crunch and even peeled diced cucumber. Toast a small finger roll or a hot dog bun, butter generously and pop the langoustine mix into its cosy new home with just a simple lettuce blanket and a maybe a few minced chives for garnish. Devour with great enjoyment.

Ingredients

250ml/ 150 grams / 1 cup cooked langoustine meat
½ a stalk of celery, washed and diced
2 Hot Dogs Buns – split top if possible
Fresh leaves of lettuce of your choice
Chives, chopped for garnish

July
—
September

Kelso Border Ridings
2nd to last Saturday
in July

Tarragon & Dijon Mayonnaise

125 ml/ 125 grams/ ½ cup light mayo
5 ml/ 5 grams/ 1 teaspoons Dijon mustard
1 dash of Tabasco Sauce
2.5 ml or 1/2 teaspoon chopped fresh tarragon leaves

Mix ingredients together, cover and refrigerated at least 1 hour before serving. Mix will keep for 3 days in the fridge. This makes more than you need for 2 filled rolls.

Instructions

- Make up Tarragon & Dijon Mayonnaise

- Cook langoustines according to instructions on packaging (depending if fresh/frozen)

- Remove cooled meat from shells and roughly chop

- In a small bowl add langoustine meat, diced celery & mayonnaise mix to taste

- Toast hot dog buns and butter if desired

- Place lettuce and half of mixture in each bun

Heaven on a roll!

*July
—
September*

Kelso Border Ridings
2nd to last Saturday
in July

The Wickerman

The Wickerman Music & Arts Festival

Last Weekend in July

The **Wickerman Music & Arts Festival** is one of the newest annual festivals and only began as recently as 2001. Based in Dundrennan in the South West of Scotland it draws much inspiration from the 1973 cult movie classic of the same name starring Christopher Lee and Edward Woodward, which was largely shot in this area and its surrounding towns.

It is a three day festival of very eclectic music and events, ending with the burning of a 40 foot wicker statue woven by local craftsmen Trevor Leat and Alex Rigg. The very apt motto for the festival is "The Wickerman Festival– it's better than it needs to be!"

The Wickerman, like **T in the Park** (1994) in Balado, Kinross, and **Belladrum** (2004) in Inverness have provided much more accessible annual hubs of music, often highlighting more local Scottish talent than the larger more established festivals such as **Glastonbury** (1970), which is located in the far reaches down south. These, and several other small but growing outdoor events give invaluable experience to a wealth of up and coming

July
—
September

The Wickerman
Festival
Last weekend in July

87

Impressive ink on display!

The lassies of summer

Lulu James

Bellohead

Fireworks and flames cap off a great three day festival!

musical talent, as well as showcasing established and even legendary talent from around the globe. Making the most of our exquisite open spaces, creative talent and our love of a very good time, may the Wickerman and other festivals take their place amongst some of the more ancient celebrations that mark not only tradtional culture, but all that is fresh, vibrant and creative about Scotland today.

July
–
September

The Wickerman
Festival
Last weekend in July

So pack up your tent, get those flowers in your hair and get ready to reconnect with your wild self as music and art give way to a fiery finale!

Venison on Flatbread with Onions, Rosemary, Horseradish & Red Currant Jam

Makes 4 Large Venision Wraps

Wild occasions call for wild food and this next glorious mess couldn't be more appropriate. After several hours of travel, music and photography, my partner-in-crime on this adventure Susan (shown posing jauntily inside the Wickerman's calf) set off in search of some nourishment. Now I confess, I could have been easily distracted by some pizza or a burger, but Susan had other plans and I am soooo glad I listened. She wanted venison and was on a mission to find some.

After much trudging through the crowd we claimed our prize venison wraps and sat down in the grass. With the gloaming upon us, the thirty foot sculpture now lit up for our viewing pleasure, we set upon this magical combination of flavours, in Susan's words, "like we were heathens!". After months of remembered craving, I have dutifully recreated this feast for the beast in you!

Ingredients:

4 Flatbread or Large Pitta Bread
60g/ 4 tablespoon Butter, half for onions, half for venison
4 Red Onions
2 Venison Haunch Steaks
Pinch of Salt & Pepper to taste
15 grams/ 15/ ml/ 1 tablespoon fresh Rosemary, minced
Creamed Horseradish to taste
Red Currant or Cranberry Jam to taste

July
—
September

The Wickerman
Festival
Last weekend in July

Instructions:

- In a large heavy skillet melt 2 tablespoons butter

- Peel onions and slice into large rounds, and cook onions on a medium to low heat, turning until soft and brown

- Pound and score the venion and fry with the other 2 tablespoons of butter for 2-3 minutes per side. Season lightly with salt & pepper and sprinkle with minced rosemary

- Lay cooked vension in a flatbread with a serving of onions and top with your choice of horseradish, red current jam or both!

An obscenely delicious feast for the wild beast in you!

The Edinburgh Military Tattoo

- August

The Edinburgh Military Tattoo is the Crown Jewel amongst the month long annual Edinburgh Festival. The term "Tattoo" derives from the Dutch term "tap toe" which was the call for last orders (literally "turn the taps off") in 18th century Flanders. The call later became a challenge for a late night competition between military bands that would round out a heavy night out.

The first Edinburgh Tattoo was performed in Princes Street Garden, which nestles underneath Edinburgh Castle, in 1949, but the official launch of the Tattoo on the Castle Esplanade was not until the following year when it joined the nascent Edinburgh Festival in 1950. This Tattoo drew approximately 6,000 visitors happy to brave the cool Edinburgh evening, seated on wooden benches on Edinburgh Castle Esplanade. The current Tattoo has become a global performance with bands and dancers from over thirty countries performing to over 220,000 people each August. It is also broadcast in over thirty countries around the globe, with annual viewing figures of over 100 million each year. It is run as a charitable organisation and has donated over £5 million over the years, particularly to the Army Benevolent Fund.

July
—
September

Edinburgh
Military Tattoo
August

93

July
—
September

Edinburgh
Military Tattoo
August

To view the Edinburgh Tattoo is a marvellously visceral as well as visual experience. Seated high up in the specially constructed bleachers that ring the Esplanade (that simply HAD to be the inspiration for JK Rowling's Quiddich stadium) whilst legions of Pipe & Drum Bands march underneath you is a rush indeed! The pomp and circumstance, the precision and the talent of the performers washes over you, as the majestic backdrop of Edinburgh Castle is lit with a never-ending light display. It is not all military bands as musicians and dancers from Thailand to Mexico to Mongolia participate in the annual event.

After the main performances, the lights are dimmed, apart from a single spotlight that illuminates a lone piper who emerges high up on the castle's ramparts. His haunting lament sets every nerve in your spine tingling. As

The view from above

the lone piper ends his tune, the evening is drawn to a close as a massive fireworks display illuminates the sky and the massed bands blast out Auld Lang Syne as they march spectacularly out of the Castle Esplanade and down the ancient cobbles of the Royal Mile.

If you thought the Changing of the Guards in the Wizard of Oz was iconic, you ain't seen nothing yet!

International performers

Smoked Salmon Nicoise

- Serves 2

There are few things in this life that I love more than a) Scottish smoked salmon and b) the fixings for a Salad Nicoise. So of course I had to combine them, topped with a classic vinaigrette, set off with a fresh lemon infused rapeseed oil dressing.

There are two performances of the Tattoo most nights with the later one not starting until 9.00 p.m. However, due to our northern location the sun rarely goes down before 9:00 p.m. making a Scottish summer day look and feel much longer: this is a blessing during Edinburgh Festival time with more opportunities to pack in even more of the amazing events on offer! After a wonderful day enjoying all that the Festival and the Fringe has to offer, this is the perfect evening meal before the rousing extravaganza of the Tattoo.

For the Salad:

500 grams/ 1lb / 6 small new potatoes, cooked until tender
2 medium eggs, hard boiled
200 grams, 1/3 lb green bean/ haricot vert, lightly steamed
200 gram/ 1/3 cup cherry tomatoes
½ red onion quartered
200 grams/ 1/3 cup black nicoise olives
250 grams/ ½ lb best quality Scottish smoked salmon
Mixed organic greens
15 grams/ 1 tablespoon capers

For the Dressing:

7 ml/ 1 clove/ 1 teaspoon garlic, minced
7 ml/ 1 teaspoon Dijon mustard
30 ml/ 2 tablespoons white wine vinegar
Salt & pepper
75 ml/ 5 tablespoon Lemon Rapeseed oil (or Olive oil)

July
—
September

Edinburgh
Military Tattoo
August

97

- Prepare each element of the salad and assemble when cooled (leftovers work great)

- In a small jar with a tight fitting lid, combine the ingredients for the dressing, shake well

- Drizzle the dressing over the various components of the salad to taste

- Serve with a crusty baguette and enjoy the long hours of the evening before taking in the Tattoo!

These are a few of my
favourite things ...

Edinburgh Fringe Festival

– August

In the first year of the Edinburgh Festival in 1947, only eight theatre companies performed at what was to become the inaugural event of the world's most successful and enduring arts festival. Seven of the groups performed in Edinburgh and one in Dunfermline in Fife. During the second year of the event a journalist from the Edinburgh Evening News commented on the increase in unofficial performers and performances at the Festival, "Round the fringe of official Festival drama, there seems to be more private enterprise than before ... I am afraid some of us are not going to be at home during the evenings!'

Thus the Fringe was named and began its journey to becoming Europe's largest arts festival, which runs for three weeks with artists from over fifty countries performing 2,500 shows in 280 venues across Edinburgh. Whilst many events are ticketed there are also non-stop free spectaculars usually up and down the Royal Mile but also spread throughout the city. You have not experienced weird until you have spent some time at the Fringe!

Of course the Edinburgh International Festival and the Fringe are now joined by concurrent events such as the Book Festival and the Film Festival, ensuring that in August, there is only one place on earth any culture vulture should be...

and that is Edinburgh!

July
–
September

Edinburgh
Fringe Festival
August

Street performance on
the Royal Mile
– Photo by Edinburgh
Festival Fringe Society

Edinburgh Fringe dancers –
Photo by Ediburgh's Festivals

Spicy Peanut Picnic Noodles

serves 4-6

The Fringe is the time to bask in the international influx of creativity that pours into Scotland each year, and also a chance to savour some warm sunshine, if you are lucky. Whilst many of the Fringe events require tickets, there are load that are free, often set in some of the city's beautiful green spaces, such as Princes Street Gardens, The Meadows, the Royal Botanic Gardens or Inverleith Park.

For the Noodles:

500 grams/ 1 lb of dried linguine
5 ml/ 1 teaspoon chilli flakes
15 ml/ 1 tablespoon toasted sesame oil

For the Dressing:

275 grams/ 1 cup chunky peanut butter
30 ml/ 2 tablespoons soy sauce
45 ml/ 3 tablespoons rice wine vinegar
15 ml/ 1 tablespoon fresh ginger, minced
15 ml/ 1 tablespoon fresh garlic, minced
175 ml/ ½ cup light oil (canola, sunflower)
15 ml/ 1 tablespoon toasted sesame oil
Juice of ½ a fresh lime

For the Salad:

2 carrots, julienned
2 courgettes/ zucchini, julienned
20 grams, ½ cup fresh coriander/ cilantro, roughly chopped
Fresh lime to garnish

*July
—
September*

Edinburgh
Fringe Festival
August

- In a large pot bring 4 litres/ 1 gallon of water to a rolling boil

- Add 1 teaspoon of chilli flakes and 1 tablespoon of toasted sesame oil

- Add the linguini and cook until al dente for approximately 8 minutes

- Drain the pasta and transfer to a large shallow bowl or tray.

- In a medium bowl combine all the ingredients for the dressing.

- Add a small amount of the dressing to the still warm noodles and toss to coat. Let cool.

- Shred or julienne the vegetables.

- When ready to serve or head out for a picnic, add the remaining dressing and vegetables. Toss well and serve with fresh lime wedges.

July
—
September

This is my sure fire crowd pleaser for any summer feast!

The Burry Man of South Queensferry

Second Friday in August

The Burry Man of South Queensferry is an ancient ritual that has been carried out by a man or 'stout lad' born in this town for hundreds of years. The specific origins of the tradition are not clear, but it has been associated with a sacrificial or scapegoat character to cleanse the town of bad luck, similar to other medieval British and European traditions. However, others suggest that is it associated with the importance of fishing in the town's history and locals draw upon a lone survivor of a wreck who protected his modesty by covering himself in burrs before asking for help. Whatever the origin, this tradition has been taking place in this town for hundreds and possibly upwards of a thousand years.

On the second Friday of August the chosen man is covered in heavy woollens, a balaclava and bowler hat that is then covered in sheets of burrs that have been gathered locally. With the addition of a flourish of flowers from a local garden, the Burry Man with his two attendants head out on their all day journey. Led by a bell ringing crier, the procession stops first at the Provost's house for a whisky and then continues on a ten hour, eight mile journey around the town, drinking whisky at multiple stops along the way.

Crowds gather along the Burry Man's route and cheer him on throughout the day, as he is joined by a piper for the last leg of his journey. It is considered very good luck to have your picture taken with the Burry Man and even to pinch a few burrs off his outfit as good luck tokens for the year to come.

The Burry Man of South Queensferry Second Friday in August

The Burryman bestowing good luck on an a newly married couple

One of endless drinks of whisky

Gathering crowds

The final leg

The Burry Man, Andrew Taylor, with his attendants Andrew Findlater & Duncan Thompson

It is a herculean feat of endurance and a wonderful (if pretty bizarre) sight to behold as the Burry Man makes his way around the houses and back to the medieval cobblestoned High Street.

Ancient, bizarre and wonderful, the Burry Man of South Queensferry is a sight to behold!

*July
—
September*

The Burry Man of
South Queensferry
Second Friday
in August

105

Grilled Oysters
with Garlic & Kale

(In honour of the return of the Native Oyster)

Serves 4

Another ancient gem from this area on the Firth of Forth is the once world reknowned Native Scottish Oyster (*Ostrea edulis*). For hundreds of years this resource was cultivated in the River Forth, and in the 13th century oyster farms in the area measured 129 square kilometres, producing upward of thirty million oysters per year. Famed for their superior quality and taste they were soon exported throughout the British Isles and to continental Europe. In fact, it was Scottish oysters that were the seed stock for much of the commercial oysters that now come from Holland. Commercial fishing and rising pollution in the 19th century led to their decline and they were declared extinct in 1957.

Since then, most of our oysters are farmed in the fresh water of Loch Ryan on the west coast, but guess what scientists have recently discovered on these salty shores...they're back! Efforts are underway to nurture these newly re-found delicacies and hopefully we will one day enjoy them again from our own waters.

So in honour of preserving the traditions and resources of the area, here is my take on Grilled Oysters Stuffed with Garlic and Kale.

Ingredients

12 large oysters in their shells
45 ml/ 45 g/ 3 tablespoons unsalted butter
45 ml/ 15 g/ 3 tablespoons dry breadcrumbs
2 cloves garlic, finely chopped
4 small shallots
250 ml or 1 cup fresh kale or spinach

July
—
September

The Burry Man of
South Queensferry
Second Friday
in August

106

50 ml or 1/4 cup white wine
15 ml/ 10 g/ 1 tablespoon soft cream cheese
Lemon wedges

- Light a BBQ or your oven grill until medium hot.

- Place the breadcrumbs in a small bowl.

- Melt the butter in a pan over medium heat. Add the garlic and cook for 1 minute taking care not to scorch.

- Add half of the melted garlic butter to the breadcrumbs and stir to combine.

- Add the shallots to the melted butter in the pan & stir for 2-3 minutes until soft.

- Stir in the white wine and reduce for 1 minute

- Add the fresh kale or spinach and stir for another 5 minutes

- Stir in soft cheese and remove from heat to cool

- Shuck the oysters as if you were serving them on the half shell, pouring out any liquor from the oysters into the nettle/spinach mixture

- Place the oysters on a baking sheet that has been prepared with a layer of salt to steady the shells

- Add 1 heaped teaspoon of the mixture to each oyster and top with breadcrumbs

- Place the oysters on the BBQ with the lid closed (or under your grill with no cover)

- Cook for about 8 minutes or until the mixture is bubbling and the breadcrumbs are a golden brown

- Remove the oysters from the heat and serve in their shells with a squeeze of fresh lemon juice

July
—
September

The Burry Man of
South Queensferry
Second Friday
in August

107

Maybe someone would even be kind enough
to slip one into the Burry Man's mouth!

Highland Games

June – September

It would not be unfair to say that the image most people have of Scotland comes from its iconic and globally popular Highland Games. The parades of Highland dancers and pipe-bands, and caber-tossing competitions attract huge gatherings of locals and tourists alike, across the country as people gather to embrace all things Scottish.

Entry to Burntisland Games

BURNTISLAND HIGHLAND GAMES
ESTABLISHED 1652
HELD ON 3rd MONDAY IN JULY
FUNDED BY
SPONSORS, DONATIONS, PROGRAMME ADVERTISMENTS

The heartbreak of weight for height

Piping competition

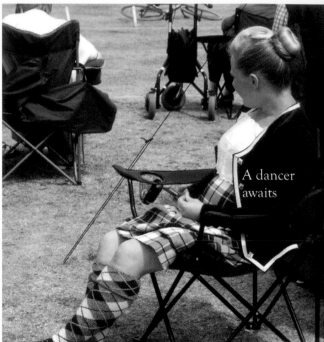

A dancer awaits

July — September

Highland Games
June – September

110

The origins of these events are ancient, with written references from the 11th Century attributing King Malcolm III with organising a race to the summit of Craig Chroinnich in Braemar. For many centuries the main events were competitions of strength and athleticism, but the modern variations encompass these and many other elements of Scottish culture such as music and dance.

Several events often go on at the one time providing spectators with a riot of colour, movement, music and cheers. And of course there are wall-to-wall bagpipes to get the blood pumping!

These are wonderful days out with family and friends and offer great opportunities to taste some local delicacies or pack your own picnic of goodies.

Raspberry Tart with Oatmeal Crumb Topping

Serves 8-12

If nothing screams Scotland like the pageantry of the Highland Games, nothing says summer to Scots themselves like fresh raspberries. This make ahead treat will be the highlight of any summer picnic.

This recipe was inspired by the foods of the Pacific Northwest, but the addition of oats and locally grown raspberries brings it straight back to this side of the Atlantic!

For the Custard:

250 grams/ 2 cups/ 8 oz ricotta cheese
Zest of 1 orange
3 medium eggs
120 grams/ ½ cup caster/granulated sugar
250 grams/ 4 cups/ 2 punnets fresh raspberries

For the Crumb Coating:

80 grams/ ½ cup butter
45 grams/ ½ cup icing/ confectioners' sugar
175 grams/ ¾ cup plain flour
50 grams rolled oats

- Preheat an oven to 180 C/ 350 F and grease a 30 cm/ 12 inch tart pan

- In a medium bowl mix together ricotta cheese, eggs, orange zest and granulated/ caster sugar

- Mix well and pour into the prepared tart pan

July

—

September

Highland Games
June – September

- Top custard with fresh raspberries

- In a medium bowl mix together butter, icing sugar, flour and oats

- Mix with fingers until it forms a crumbly dry mix

- Scatter crumb coating over raspberries and custard and bake for 35 – 45 minutes or until a toothpick comes out clean

- Cool tart completely before serving. The tart can be chilled for several hours or overnight

- Dust with icing sugar before serving

July

–

September

Highland Games
June – September

The Embodiment of
Scottish Summertime

Summer Ends, Autumn Arrives

While summer can sometimes be more of a technical term rather than a season in Scotland, autumn is often simply glorious. The fresh crispness returns to the air and the shadows grow long but there is still warmth to be had in the sunshine.

As the children return to school in mid-August the gaiety of the dog days has long given way to new routines and schedules. But while shoes and pencils are fresh inside, outside this is also the time for harvest. Everything from oats, wheat and corn come in, but most notably is the potato harvest. In Scotland the potato harvest is known as "Tattie Howking" with "tattie" being potato and "to howk" literally means to pull from the ground. To this day schools schedule a two week break, ostensibly to be available to help with the harvest, but most of us are happy to take the holiday and get out into Scotland's beautiful mountains to mark the occasion instead!

This is a great time of year to catch your breath after the festivities from the summer and before the Christmas season (which starts about November 1st!). Many Scots seem to instinctively crave the returning darkness as a time to draw back inside and rest for a moment.

Just to point out the obvious, given our very mild temperatures it can easy to forget just how northerly our location is. However, the dramatic difference between the lightness of the summer months and the sheer speed at how fast it all changes to darkness can be that short sharp reminder that yes indeed, we are on the same latitude as Moscow!

So as the months of midnight sun and intense blue skies soon succumb to inky blackness with the clocks turning back, Scots start to get cosy. Away goes the BBQ and out comes the soup pot, but the fun is set to continue!

July
—
September

Fireworks for Guy Fawkes Night

October
–
December

National Mod choral group

Royal National Mod

Mid October

The term *mod* means assembly or gathering in Gaelic but has since become known to mean a large annual competition for Gaelic music, song, literature, arts and sporting competitions.

The largest of these is the Royal National Mod, a week-long celebration of Gaelic culture.

The Royal National Mod is run by *An Comunn Gàidhealach* (The Gaelic Association) and was first held in Oban in 1891. The concert was attended by many nobles of the day including the Princess Royal, Duchess of Fife. Since 1892 the Mod has been held in October of each year, only being suspended twice, during the two World Wars. The term "Royal" is a recent intervention and was added when Queen Elizabeth II became its patron.

The Mod is mostly organised into formal competitions for Gaelic music, song, literature and poetry. It also sponsors the annual Mod Cup for Shinty, a Gaelic Sport not entirely unlike field hockey, but the players can block and tackle. The winners from each of the day's events are invited to perform at the Winner's Ceilidh each evening.

October
—
December

Royal
National Mod
Mid October

117

The awards!

I was lucky enough to attend the evening of the Final Concert which featured many of the Gold Medal winners. The music and songs were alternately haunting and rousing, and whilst I was a wee bit adrift as I am not a Gaelic speaker I can say it was a privilege to see that much talent in a live performance.

The Mod is hugely popular and as such draws large crowds. An independent gathering of musicians and artists events has also sprung up around the official Mod and is referred to as the Mod Fringe, similar to the Edinburgh Fringe.

These Fringe events are sometimes known as the "Whisky Olympics", a term that can be taken as a slur or a badge of honour depending on the context!

October
—
December

Royal
National Mod
Mid October

Mussels with White Wine, Shallots & Parsley

Serves 2 Generously

As Oban was the location of the first Mod, I thought I would include some of the wonderful shellfish that comes ashore there today. Mussels are one of the easiest ways to enjoy the succulent fruits of the sea and probably one of my favourite dishes for feeling like I am harbour side.

Everything about the Mod felt authentic and elegant, so I chose the very simplest way to prepare these gems to convey the same characteristics. Don't wait to go to a restaurant to enjoy these goodies, once you make them at home it may well become a fast favourite of yours as well!

Ingredients:

1 kilo, 2 pounds live mussels
350 ml, 1½ cups, ½ bottle white wine
30 grams, 2 tablespoon butter, melted
3 medium shallots, diced small
2 cloves, 1 teaspoon garlic, minced
30 grams, 1 cup fresh parsley, chopped
1 baguette, sliced and toasted

- Thoroughly rinse the mussels and remove the beards

- Discard any mussels that are cracked and any that do not close tightly when tapped

- Scrub any seaweed off the shells with a never been used scouring sponge

- In a large skillet/ fry pan melt the butter and gently sauté the shallots and garlic for 2-3 minutes

- In a large lidded pot place the wine, cover and bring to boil

October
—
December

Royal
National Mod
Mid October

119

- Put the mussels into the steaming wine, cover and cook for 3-5 minutes or until shells open

- Add the butter, shallot & garlic mix to the shells with a large handful of the parsley and stir to mix

- Spoon the mussels into two large bowls discarding any that didn't open

- Pour the remaining cooking liquor over the mussels and finish with remaining parsley

- Serve with toasted baguette slices for a heavenly treat!

Keeping it classic, elegant & delicious!

Halloween

31st October

In the Celtic calendar, Samhuinn (Summers-end) or Halloween together with Beltane (p.62) were the two most important festivals. It not only marked the passage of summer and harvest time but as the Celtic year is believed to begin with winter, it was literally the New Year as well.

As the dark nights descend and the trees begin to shed their leaves, this is the time where it it believed that the veil between the world of the living and the dead is thinnest...

... and you must protect yourself from spirits, witches, fairies and trolls.

Halloween
guisers

Halloween
31st October

121

Traditional turnip
(tumshee) lanterns

To protect themselves from the surfeit of spirits, children would carve lanterns out of turnips with garish faces to protect them as they took part in the much anticipated *guising* (going door to door in disguise) to be rewarded with apples, coins and hazelnuts. Parties often include fun rituals that are believed to be relics of Druidism such as dooking (dunking) for apples and fortune telling.

Modern Halloween in Scotland looks very much like its Americanised cousin with candy and monster masks, and pumpkins replacing the traditional turnip or Tumshie lantern, but you must be scary, no cute Minnie Mouse outfits! Another difference is that all children prepare a joke, song or trick to perform before being awarded the sweet treat, a simple call of "Trick or Treat" will not produce any of the goods!

Turnip & Pear Soup with Fried Sage

Serves 4

In my youth in the States, Halloween always meant toasted pumpkin seeds and most likely pumpkin bread to follow in the days after. Faced with a rather large store of turnip scrapings I turned to my seasonal favourites of pear and sage to create this surprisingly light and floral soup. It has passed the picky kid test so I thought I would push it a bit and add a super tasty garnish of 'Witches Fingers' also known as delicious fried sage leaves.

Ingredients:

1 medium, 800 gram, 2 ½ cups (or inside of 3) turnip, peeled & diced
15 ml, 1 tablespoon olive oil
½ medium onion, 175 ml, ½ cup diced
2 ripe pears, de-stemmed & deseeded, peels are ok, diced
1500 ml, 4 cups water
2 vegetable bouillon cubes or 2 teaspoons loose powder bouillion
15 ml, 1 tablespoon butter, for sage
12-15 fresh sage leaves for garnish

- In a pot sauté the diced onions in 1 tablespoon olive oil on a low heat for 3-5 minutes

- Add turnip, pear, vegetable stock cubes and water

- Bring to boil and then reduce to simmer uncovered for 30 minutes

- Blend with an immersion blender until smooth

- Add salt and pepper to taste

- When ready to serve melt the butter in a small sauté/ fry pan

- Place the fresh sage leaves face down one at time into the butter for 30 seconds

- Turn leaves over and cook them flat on the other side

- Remove from pan and drain on kitchen roll/ paper towel

- Garnish each bowl with magic number three to ward off witches!

A good use of the carved turnip and a lovely soup to soothe even the most over-excited of children.

Bonfire Night

"Remember, remember the 5th of November, the gunpowder treason and plot. I know of no reason why the gunpowder treason should ever be forgot."

Guy Fawkes Night, more widely known as **Bonfire Night**, is when people up and down Britain gather in the frosty blackness of a November night to celebrate the joyous relief of an event that never happened. The story in a nutshell is this; in 1605 a group of conspirators got together and planned to blow up the Houses of Parliament in London by stacking barrels of gunpowder in the cellar. In doing so, they planned to kill King James I of England VI of Scotland and his entire Court, and install his daughter Elizabeth to the throne. The fuse lighter-to be, one Guy or rather "Guido" Fawkes, was caught, tortured and while scheduled to be hung, drawn and quartered, managed to jump to his death from the steps of the gallows. Everyone else involved in the plot was gathered up and a major act of terrorism was averted.

The problems stemmed from the first joining of the Crowns between England and Scotland when King James V1 of Scotland ascended the throne of England. At the heart of all the trouble seemed to be religious differences and tensions, but modern historians have suggested that in addition to these, the new King had made himself very unpopular as he had completely replaced everyone in power in London with his Scottish cohorts and was not making himself welcome in certain circles.

Whatever the motivation, be it religious, political, tribal or all of the above, thankfully a serious bloodbath was thwarted. The immediate legacy of the averted crisis was that as the news of the plot spread, people were encouraged

Burntisland Bonfire

to light bonfires to celebrate the foiled efforts to assassinate the King, and that an Act of Parliament designated the 5th of November as a day to give thanks for "the joyful day of deliverance" from the near disaster.

On the first anniversary of the plot in 1606, a sermon of thanks was held at the Court of King James VI & I (later of the King James Bible fame), that was to become the origins of the **"Remember, Remember the 5th of November"** nursery rhyme.

These events are marked across Great Britain with sparklers, fireworks, bonfires and parties.

October

—

December

Bonfire
5th November

It is a really fun event that feels very defiant against the sudden darkness of the nights and really brings the community spirit alive!

Vegetarian Chilli with Cheese & Corn Chips

Serves Six

For reasons that no one seems to viably answer, it has become rather a modern tradition to serve chilli on Bonfire Night. Most likely because it is hearty and warming and can be made in advance to welcome guests home after the fireworks displays. If you are feeling even more adventurous, get a sturdy cooler from summertime and pack it full of hay. Place your hot pot of chilli in with its lid and you can bring the hot feast to the fire yourself!

Whenever I am preparing for a meal where I am likely to spontaneously invite people over after an event, I like to include a vegetarian option. It just makes everyone feel welcome, and with this one you don't even have to tell the meat eaters that it is veggie!

Ingredients

1 large onion, diced
1 red pepper, diced
250 ml, 100 grams, 1 cup corn, fresh or frozen
1 can/tin, 330 ml, kidney beans, rinsed
2 cloves, 2 teaspoon garlic, minced
330 grams, 2 ½ cups Quorn Mince (vegetarian protein) or ground beef if non-veggie
3 cans/tins of chopped tomatoes
2 cubes, 2 teaspoons vegetable bouillon
15 ml, 1 tablespoon Brewer's Yeast (Marmite)
7 ml, 1 teaspoon salt
3.5 ml/ ½ teaspoon pepper
7 ml, 1 teaspoon oregano, dried

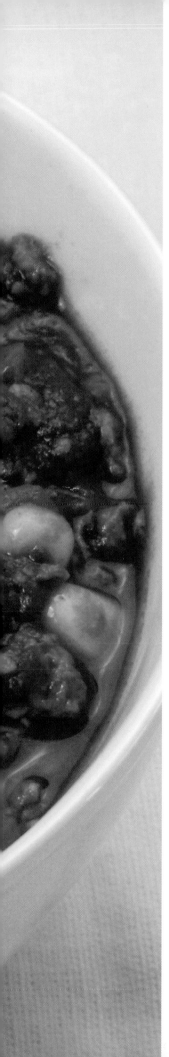

3.5 ml/ ½ teaspoon chipotle pepper – optional
3.5 ml/ ½ teaspoon paprika
3.5 ml/ ½ teaspoon cayenne pepper
3.5 ml/ ½ teaspoon cumin
3.5 ml// ½ teaspoon coriander (dried)
7 ml, 1 teaspoon salt
3.5 ml, ½ teaspoon black pepper
500 ml, 2 cups grated cheese
1 large bag plain corn tortillas

- In a large pot heat a small drizzle of olive or sunflower oil, add diced onion, peppers & corn.

- Stir for 3-5 minutes on medium heat to soften

- Add vegetarian mince if using or regular mince (ground beef) if non-veggie

- Sauté for 3 minutes

- Add the rest of the ingredients and bring to the boil

- Reduce heat to simmer and cook for 30 minutes, stirring often

- Can be made ahead and freezes well

- Serve piping hot and garnish with grated cheese and lots of corn tortilla chips.

A Warm and Welcoming Treat for Everyone to Enjoy!

October

–

December

Bonfire
5th November

129

St Andrew's Day

– 30th November

As the Patron Saint of Scotland, St Andrew's is a day to break out all things Scottish and seriously kick up your heels!

The man behind the myth, Andrew himself was rumoured to be a Galilean fisherman and one of Jesus' apostles. When sentenced to death by crucifiction by the Romans in Greece, he requested to be hung on a diagonal cross as he did not believe he was worthy of dying in the same way as Jesus. Part of his remains (or relics) were said to have been brought to Scotland by St. Regulus, a monk from Patras in Greece in 345 AD, and landed at a Pictish settlement that would later become the site of St. Andrew's Cathedral in Fife.

The Beehive Inn,
Grassmarket, Edinburgh

The view of Edinburgh Castle,
St Andrew's Day

The legend continues in 832 AD when the Pictish King Fergus led an army
of Picts and Scots against the Angles, led by their leader Aethelstan, near
present day Athelstansford in East Lothian. Appealing to St. Andrew, Fergus
vowed that if he was victorious he would honour Andrew as Patron Saint
of Scotland. As the morning dawned with a clear blue sky, white clouds
forming a huge X appeared above the warriors. Fergus was victorious and
not only adopted St Andrew as the Patron Saint but also claimed the white
diagonal cross against the blue background as the Flag of Scotland. Now
known as the Saltire, it is believed to be the oldest national flag in Europe.

131

Since 2006, St. Andrew's day has become an official bank holiday and enjoys an ever increasing surge of parades, concerts, parties and of course ceilidhs (pronounced kay-lees) of traditional music and dancing. This year I joined the crowds in Edinburgh's Grassmarket to enjoy a full day and evening of events. Whilst very important in its own right, it is also the start of the marathon of Scotland's winter festivals that last right through to the end of January!

St Andrew's Day bandstand

St. Andrew's Day Roast Lamb with Spiced Potatoes

Serves 4-6

Whilst St. Andrew is celebrated on the 30th of November as the Patron Saint in Scotland, he is also the Patron Saint of Greece, Russia and even Barbados! This is a day to celebrate all day long, and what better way than a hearty roast leg of lamb for guests to help themselves. I couldn't resist a culinary nod to our Patron Saint cousins, so enjoy your lamb with a bit of Greek flavouring, some Allspice potatoes, served with Tzatziki and Beetroot relish for the full cultural compliments of St. Andrew!

Ingredients:

For the Lamb:

15 ml/ 1 tablespoon dried oregano
15 ml/ 1 tablespoon dried rosemary
45 ml/ 3 tablespoons olive oil
Zest & juice of 1 lemon
5 grams/ 2 teaspoons salt
4 cloves, 15 ml/ 1 tablespoon garlic, minced
1.5 kilo/ 3 lbs leg of lamb – bone in

For the Allspice Potatoes

500 grams/ 1lb baby potatoes
30 ml/ 2 tablespoons olive oil
7 ml/ 1 teaspoon dried oregano
15 ml/ 1 tablespoon Allspice
7 ml/ 1 teaspoon sea salt
3.5 ml/ ½ teaspoon cracked black pepper

Happy Saint
Andrew's Day!

For the Tzatziki:

250 ml/ 1 cup thick Greek Yoghurt
25 grams/ ½ cup cucumber, seeded & diced
7 ml/ 1 teaspoon fresh lemon juice
7 grams/ 2 tablespoons fresh mint leaves, minced
Salt & Pepper to taste

For the Beetroot Relish

2 beetroots, cooked, peeled and julienned
15 ml/ 2 tablespoons red wine vinegar
7 ml/ 2 teaspoons fresh dill, chopped
Salt & pepper to taste.

For the Lamb

- Preheat an oven to 180 C/ 350 F

- Mix everything but the lamb together and coat the leg of lamb generously

- Set aside for 30 minutes.

For the Allspice Potatoes

- Place the potatoes in a large baking dish with sides

- Add all the remaining ingredients and toss to coat thoroughly

- Place the leg of lamb on top of the potatoes and place dish into the oven for approximately 45minutes to 1 hour. Lamb is done when it is 50 C/ 150 F. Use an instant read thermometer for best results. Remove from oven, cover with foil and rest for 15-20 minutes

- While the lamb is cooking, in one bowl prepare the Tzatziki, and in another bowl prepare the Beetroot Relish. Store in the refrigerator until ready to serve.

- When there is a suitable break between music and dance call your guest to the table or buffet for what will surely be most welcome refreshments!

Christmas
in
Edinburgh

The Scots go in for Christmas in a huge way, which is somewhat surprising considering its centuries long abolishment from Scottish life. When the Protestant Reformation took Scotland by storm in 1560, all Christian feasting days were frowned upon, but Christmas most of all. Gone were the previous celebrations of Yule which usually involved gift-giving, dancing music and merriment and in came the Act of Parliament that not only banned Christmas but also banned any work holidays at that time of year! This lasted until 1712 when, after the Union with England, Wales and Ireland it was repealed by an Act of Parliament in Westminster. Even so, Christmas remained incredibly low key in Scotland because of the lasting influence of the Kirk and only became a public holiday in 1958 with Boxing Day joining it in 1974!

So, from the 16th to the 20th century all Yuletide and Christmas traditions and festivities were enthusiastically transferred to the New Year celebration of Hogmanay. It is only in the past few decades that Christmas has once again blossomed, and instead of diminishing the other winter celebrations, it has just expanded the entire season into one long party.

Christmas is a fabulous time of year, but in Edinburgh in particular it is magical.

The Ferris Wheel over Princes Street

The city is beautiful as it is, but bedecked in fairy lights set against the inky blackness of the winter sky, and crowned with the spectacular German Market nestling underneath the Castle crag, it is breathtaking. The market runs from November to Christmas Eve with fairground rides, food, crafts, an outdoor ice-rink and even reindeer!

October – December

Christmas in Edinburgh

It is beyond story-book beautiful and is sure to put a little Christmas magic into the heart of the most hardened Scrooge.

138

The Carousel at the Christmas Market

The Fairy Lights & Train Ride in the Gardens, Edinburgh

Pheasant, Bacon & Port Bridies

Serves 6

Why pheasant? Why not! It is literally the bounty of the county, packed with nutrition and more likely to have led a good life rather than farmed poultry. It has a deep rich flavour with a meatier consistency than chicken that holds up well to bold flavours. I was also pleasantly surprised to find each pheasant cost no more than £5.00, bringing the price in line with an organic chicken.

"Bridie" is a term that originated in Forfar in the 1850s and got its name from its frequent appearance on wedding menus. It is similar to a Cornish Pasty but does not contain potatoes. This Bridie is a wonderful combination of the finest of restaurant flavours with the price and portability of most quality pies.

Ingredients:

1 pheasant (can be found at a Farm Shop or online from Game websites)
1 red onion, sliced in half
3 bay leaves
2 cups Port
30 ml, 1tablespoon butter
3 slices smoked bacon
100 grams, 1 cup chestnut mushrooms, diced large
Salt and pepper
2 sheets ready-rolled puff pastry
1 egg for brushing pastry

For the filling:

- In a slow cooker, place ½ red onion sliced into rings

- Use onions as a bed and place the pheasant on top

This is a richer, more flavourful,
sexy cousin of Coq au Vin all
wrapped up in a portable puff
pastry for easy strolling through
the holiday markets.

- Place bay leaves, 1 cup of Port and a dash of salt and pepper

- Cover and cook on low for 5 hours

- When cooked, remove pheasant and let cool

- Strain cooking liquor & discard (or reserve for future poultry gravy)

- Once cooled, separate meat from skin & bones

- Dice meat and set aside, discard skin & bone

For the Bridies:

- Preheat an oven to 200 C/ 400 F

- In a saucepan cook the bacon slices

- Once cooked remove from pan to drain, dice when cooled

- In the same pan as the bacon, sauté/fry ½ red onion and sliced mushrooms for 5 minutes. Remove from pan

- In a large bowl combine cooked and diced pheasant, bacon, onions & mushroom

- Deglaze the sauté/ fry pan with 1 cup of Port. Simmer until reduced to syrup consistency. Pour over filling mix

- Roll out the puff pastry and place 50 grams/ ½ cup of the filling in each

- Fold pastry over the filling, cut to shape and crimp edges with fork to seal

- Place on a greased baking sheet, repeat until filling & pastry are finished

- Brush each Bridie with egg wash and bake for 10-15 minutes until puffed and brown

- Serve piping hot!

Trio Of Traditional Scottish Treats For Hogmanay

Shortbread, Tablet & Macaroons

Serves 12

Traditional Hogmanay baking including shortbread, tablet and macaroons

And so we have come around the calendar to Hogmanay once again. Preparations for the New Year are serious business as you need to ensure as much good luck comes to you as possible. So, the house needs cleaning, washing done, torn things mended and borrowed things returned. It is also the time you get out your Granny's recipes for some traditional Scottish sweets that will transport any Scot back to their childhood.

The first is Shortbread which is available in many parts of the globe. With only three ingredients it is easy to overlook, but do not be blasé about this tender, crumbly delicacy. The second is Tablet, but many might think of it as light fudge. It is rocket powered sweetness and should melt in your mouth. This is one of the few things that is sweet enough to satiate the famous Scots' sweet-tooth! The last is a chocolate and coconut macaroon. This one is different to other confectionary known by the same name, in that is it made with mashed potatoes (for real!). Each of these appear very simple but don't be fooled. Scottish baking can sometimes be a dark art requiring a Granny's experience or some serious skill, but hopefully these recipes will provide relatively straight forward ways to achieve happy results.

As the midnight hour approaches, the head of the house should open the back door and let out the Old Year. The door should be closed right before the bells toll and then the front door should be flung open to welcome the New Year. Kisses and shouts join in the noise and sometimes pots and pans are still banged to ward off any of the other-worldly creatures that may be afoot at this special time. A rousing round of Auld Lang Syne caps off the welcome and the First Footers begin to arrive.

A New Year is born, another celebration ensues and all in this rich, warm and wacky nation begin another year of merriment.

Shortbread

Ingredients:

500 ml/ 2 cups plain flour
125 ml/ ½ cup caster (granulated) sugar
115g/ 4 oz/ ¾ cup butter

- Preheat the oven to 130 C/ 270 F

- Grease either an 8" x 12" (20cm x 32cm) rectangular tray or a 8" (20cm) round tart pan

October

—

December

Hogmany
27th December
- 2nd January

144

- (Make your life easier on both counts and use trays with removable bottoms)

- Generously grease whichever pan you choose

- In a large bowl combine all three ingredients and mix with fingertips until it resembles coarse crumbs

- When the mixture comes together press it into the tart pan (the recipes make 2 8" rounds)

- Score into desired portions and prick with a fork to decorate

- Bake for 35 – 45 minutes until there is the slightest browning around the edges

- Remove from heat and cool completely

Fool Proof Tablet

(This recipe was kindly given to me by Marion Scott at the Tomb of the Eagles in Orkney)

Ingredients:

500 grams/ 1 lb icing/ powdered sugar
60 grams/ ¼ cup/ 4 oz butter
30 ml/ 2 tablespoons syrup (golden or maple will do)
1 cup condensed milk

- Prepare 2 separate 8 x 12 trays, heavily greased

- Add all the ingredients into a large microwave safe bowl

- Microwave (700W) on Defrost for 2 x 5 minute intervals, stirring between

- Microwave for 5 additional minutes on high keeping an eye out for when it rises

- Stop and stir down at least twice in that 5 minutes

October
—
December

Hogmany
27th December
- 2nd January

145

- Working quickly, pour the mixture into one of the prepared trays, spreading evenly to the edges

- The mixture will set very fast so when cool enough to touch, cut into small squares with a knife or cutter

- Remove cut squares and place on the other tray to cool completely

Mandy's Macaroon – From the Heaven Sent Mandy Wilkie

175 grams/ ½ cup/ 4 oz cooled mashed potatoes
500 grams/ 1 1b icing/ powedered sugar
250 grams/ ½ lb/ 98 oz plain chocoate for melting
250 ml/ ½ cup/ 4 oz dessicated/ shredded coconut

- Prepare potatoes for mashing or just use left overs, add all the sugar until it is a sticky dough

- On a large baking tray with greaseproof paper roll the dough into small logs or balls

- Place in freezer for 30 minutes

- Lightly toast the coconut and place in a bowl

- Melt the chocolate and place in a bowl

- Working quickly take the cold dough balls and roll in the melted chocolate and then coat in coconut – set aside to firm (may need to be returned to freezer for 30 more minutes)

October

—

December

Hogmany
27th December
- 2nd January

Happy Hogmanay!